C0-AWT-460

THE U.S. FEDERAL BUDGET PROCESS

AN OVERVIEW AND GLOSSARY OF TERMS

LIBRARY
RESOURCES FOR THE FUTURE, INC.

THE U.S. FEDERAL BUDGET PROCESS

AN OVERVIEW AND GLOSSARY OF TERMS

Edited by
G. I. Maltese

LIBRARY
RESOURCES FOR THE FUTURE, INC

NOVA SCIENCE PUBLISHERS, INC.

Art Director: Christopher Concannon
Graphics: Elenor Kallberg and Maria Ester Hawrys
Manuscript Coordinator: Roseann Pena
Book Production: Tammy Sauter, Benjamin Fung
and Michelle Lalo
Circulation: Irene Kwartiroff and Annette Hellinger

*Library of Congress Cataloging–in–Publication Data
available upon request*

ISBN 1-56072-192-8

© *1995 Nova Science Publishers, Inc.*
  6080 Jericho Turnpike, Suite 207
  Commack, New York 11725
  Tele. 516-499-3103 Fax 516-499-3146
  E Mail Novasci1@aol.com

All rights reserved. No part of this book may be reproduced, stored in a retrieval system or transmitted in any form or by any means: electronic, electrostatic, magnetic, tape, mechanical, photocopying, recording or otherwise without permission from the publishers.

Printed in the United States of America

CONTENTS

INTRODUCTION

The federal budget is the primary policy statement of the President's fiscal priorities and proposals for allocating expenditures and taxes. The budget also functions as a framework and reference point for congressional actions. Because of the budget's economic, social, and political importance and its role in providing the information needed to assess program efficiency and effectiveness, an understanding of budget concepts is important to anyone interested in how the United States Government works or does not work. Budgetary terms and definitions must also be understood in order to consider and implement changes in the budgetary or financial management process and to grasp what the government is doing at any given point in time.

This book is a basic reference document for the Congress, federal agencies, and others interested in the federal budget-making process. It emphasizes budget terms, but relevant economic and accounting terms are also defined to help the user appreciate the dynamics of the budget process. It distinguishes between any differences in budgetary and nonbudgetary meanings of terms.

This small book is distilled from a GAO publication - "Budget Glossary." We have tried to arrange the materials, edit terms, and add commentary whenever appropriate for ease of use and access to the information.

OVERVIEW OF THE FEDERAL BUDGET PROCESS

A budget, in customary usage, is a plan for managing funds, setting levels of spending, and financing the spending. Specifically, it presents receipt and spending estimates and recommendations. Since formulating a budget involves choosing among alternative expenditures, a budget is also a plan of operations and a description of goals and priorities. The federal budget contains

- a record of actual receipts and spending levels for the fiscal year just completed,
- a record of current-year estimated receipts and spending, and
- estimated receipts and spending for the upcoming fiscal year and 4 years beyond.

While federal budgeting is a continuous process, it is possible to identify a 2-1/2 year cycle. This cycle can be understood and studied in terms of four phases:

(1) **executive budget formulation,**
(2) **the congressional budget process,**
(3) **budget execution and control,** and
(4) **audit and evaluation.**

The discussion that follows describes the budgetary process in general and then in terms of these four phases.

The federal budget process is initiated by executive budget formulation. By law, the President prepares and submits the executive budget to the Congress. The Congress reviews the President's budget and then adopts its budget resolution which sets forth its budget guidelines. Subsequently, the Congress and the President enact laws that create levels of budgetary authority - the legal right to obligate and ultimately spend funds-which become legally binding spending ceilings for all federal agencies.

The Constitution gives the Congress the responsibility for passing substantive law (that is, law that authorizes programs), appropriations, and tax legislation (Article I, sections 1, 8, and 9) and effectively gives the President executive responsibilities (Article II). However, there was no formal budgeting system when the Budget and Accounting Act of 1921 established a federal budget process that requires the President to transmit a proposed federal budget to the Congress for the upcoming fiscal year. The Congressional Budget Act of 1974 created the congressional budget process and established October 1 through September 30 as the federal fiscal year.

PHASE 1: EXECUTIVE BUDGET FORMULATION

By February, the President submits to the Congress a budget for the fiscal year starting on the following October 1. Preparation of the budget begins about 10 months before it is submitted to the Congress. For example, for the 1993 budget, transmitted to the Congress in February of 1992, the budget process began in the spring of 1991. Thus federal agencies must deal concurrently with 3 fiscal years: (1) the current year, whose budget they are executing, (2) the coming fiscal year beginning October 1, for which they are seeking funds (the budget year), and (3) the following fiscal year, for which they are preparing information and requests.

Executive budget formulation, based upon proposals, evaluations, and policy decisions, begins at agencies' organizational units. During executive budget formulation, federal agencies receive revenue estimates and economic projections from the Treasury Department, the Council of Economic Advisers (CEA), and the Office of Management and Budget (OMB).

EXECUTIVE BUDGET FORMULATION TIMETABLE

April-June: OMB and the President conduct reviews to establish policy for the next budget

During April through June, before it examines detailed spending and program requests, OMB reviews the major policy issues for the next budget and updates the long-term forecast of receipts and expenditures. Together with the Department of the Treasury and CEA, it presents the President with a projection of economic conditions. The President then makes policy decisions while OMB issues technical instructions for preparing the annual budget-year estimate and the estimates for the following 4 fiscal years. For example, in the April-June 1991 timeframe, OMB issued instructions for making 1993-97 budget estimates.

July-August: OMB provides agencies with policy guidance for the upcoming budget

Based on the President's decisions during policy development, OMB, in July and August, issues policy directions and planning ceilings to the agencies, both for the budget year and for the following 4 years. These instructions guide the preparation of agencies' formal budget requests. In July and August 1991, these instructions and ceilings applied to the 1993-97 budget estimates.

September-October: Agencies submit initial budget request materials

Executive branch departments and agencies subject to executive branch budget review must submit their budget requests and other initial materials to OMB by September 1 of the year prior to the start of the year that the budget request covers (that is, September 1,1992 for fiscal year 1994). OMB representatives then schedule hearings or informal discussions with agencies to obtain a better understanding of agency policies and programs and to allow agencies to defend their requests. Agencies not subject to executive branch review (for example, the Federal Reserve Board) submit their budget request by October 15 of the year prior to the year that the budget request covers (for example, October 15, 1992 for fiscal year 1994). The legislative and judiciary branches submit their budget materials in November and December of that year, in accordance with OMB guidance.

November-December: OMB and presidential decisions

OMB reviews the agencies' materials and its staff prepares issue papers and recommendations for the OMB Director's Review. Then, the staff discuss major issues with the Director. After the Director's Review, OMB passes budget decisions back to the agencies. They may appeal decisions with which they disagree. If OMB and an agency cannot reach agreement, the agency may appeal to the President.

Final budget decisions will also reflect proposals for management and program delivery improvements resulting from agency and OMB reviews during the executive budget formulation process. One section of the *Budget of the United States Government, Fiscal Year 1993,* "Managing for Integrity and Efficiency," highlights these proposals.

OMB not only assists in making individual budget decisions, it also tracks the result of these decisions. OMB calculates the effect of budget decisions on receipts, budget authority, and outlays.

When OMB informs agencies of final decisions, agencies revise their budget submissions to conform to these decisions. These final estimates are transmitted to the Congress in the President's budget.

By the first Monday in February: President submits budget

In accordance with current law, the President must transmit the budget to the Congress on or before the first Monday in February.

January-February: OMB sends allowance letters

After transmitting the budget to the Congress, OMB sends allowance letters to agency heads to formally inform them of:

(1) **budget decisions and multiyear planning estimates,**
(2) **employment ceilings,**
(3) **goals for management improvements,** and
(4) **significant policy, program, and administrative matters.**

The multiyear planning estimates become the starting point in formulating the President's next budget.

By July 15: President submits mid-session review document to the Congress

The Congressional Budget Act of 1974, as amended, requires the President to submit to the Congress on or before July 15 a supplementary budget summary which provides data to aid in an evaluation of the President's budget. This summary, referred to as the **mid-session review**, includes updated Presidential policy budget estimates, summary updates to the information contained in the budget submission, and budget-year baseline estimates.

PHASE 2: THE CONGRESSIONAL BUDGET PROCESS

The Congress does not have to adopt the President's budget proposals and may alter them or make its own proposals. If fact most congresses use the President's budget as a starting point only. It can and does change funding levels, modify or eliminate programs (or add new ones not requested by the President), and act on legislation determining tax rates. The Congress, however, normally does not vote on expenditures (outlays) of federal funds directly, but rather on requests for budget authority. Budget authority permits federal agencies to incur obligations and hence to spend federal funds. The Congress does not enact a congressional budget, but rather has a budget process that yields legislation authorizing and appropriating funds within the guidelines of a budget resolution. OMB compiles the permitted levels of spending determined by authorization and appropriation laws and shows them in the next year's executive budget documents as estimated budget levels for the current fiscal year.

Before an agency requests budget authority, the Congress generally acts on legislation authorizing the agency to carry out a particular program, such as monitoring toxic waste cleanup or building highways. In the case of borrowing authority, contract authority, and the authority to obligate and expend the proceeds of offsetting receipts and collections, authorizing legislation creates budget authority, subject to limitations expressed in appropriations laws. Authorizing legislation may or may not limit the funds for a given program. Some programs are reauthorized every year, while other programs are authorized for several years advance.

For those programs for which funds are provided through the appropriations process, the amount each department, agency, or program receives is determined by legislation considered by the House and Senate Appropriations Committees and their subcommittees, each of which has jurisdiction over specific federal agencies or programs. Less than 40 percent of federal expenditures are controlled by appropriations committees. (For further explanation, see the definitions of Backdoor Authority, Budget Authority, Obligational Authority, Outlay, and Spending Authority.)

Appropriations may be for 1 year (the standard form), which allows an agency to obligate funds only during 1 fiscal year; they may be multiyear appropriations; or they may be "no-year," that is, they may be for any fiscal year. The Constitution requires that all revenue (tax) bills originate in the House, and, by custom, the House also originates appropriations measures.

When an agency does not receive its new appropriation before the old one lapses, it must cease ongoing, regular functions unless their cessation would immediately threaten the safety of human life or the protection of property, or unless a **continuing resolution** is passed by the Congress and presented to the President. The President may veto the resolution, sign it into law, or allow it to become law without signing it.

In 1974, both the design of the federal budget and the process were changed. The Congressional Budget Act of 1974 established the current functional structure of the budget and created congressional budget procedures and institutions to support a new congressional budget process. The Balanced Budget and Emergency Deficit Control Act of

1985,[1] as amended by the Balanced Budget and Emergency Deficit Control Reaffirmation Act of 1987 and the Budget Enforcement Act of 1990, established procedures designed to force a reduction in the federal deficit.

ESTABLISHMENT OF THE CONGRESSIONAL BUDGET PROCESS

To create a congressional budget process, the Congressional Budget Act of 1974 created new institutions: the Senate and House Budget Committees and the Congressional Budget Office (CBO). The act gives the Budget Committees of the Senate and the House authority to draft the concurrent resolution on the budget (Congress's annual budget plan for the federal government) for consideration by the full Senate and House. Unlike the authorizing and appropriating committees, which focus on individual federal programs, the Budget Committees focus on broad spending categories, aggregate federal budget totals, and how total spending affects the national economy. The Committees also keep track of individual authorizations, appropriations, and revenue decisions that the Congress makes during the budget process. CBO provides economic and program analyses and cost information on existing and proposed federal programs to Members of the Congress involved in the budget process, the Budget Committees, and other committees. The Impoundment Control Act of 1974 (Title X of the Congressional Budget and Impoundment Control Act) requires that any budget authority the executive branch proposes to defer or rescind (see the definitions of Deferral of Budget Authority and Rescission) must be reported to the Congress. Rescissions, which are executive branch decisions not to spend funds, do not take effect unless they are approved by both Houses within 45 days of continuous session of the President's notification.

The Congressional Budget Act of 1974, as amended, established the following congressional budget process. The Congress, before it enacts any budget legislation, must adopt a concurrent budget resolution to guide its considerations of appropriations and tax measures. In the absence of a budget resolution, a point of order may be raised against appropriations acts. (For more information, see the definition of Point of Order.) The resolution sets target totals, covering the budget year and the next 4 years, for budget authority, outlays, receipts, the surplus or deficit, and the public debt.[2] The resolution also subdivides the targets into functional spending categories, such as defense and health.

---

[1] Otherwise known as Gramm-Rudman-Hollings.

[2] Under the Budget Enforcement Act of 1990, the resolution must set forth the appropriate level for the budget year and each of the succeeding 4 years.

The act provides for increases or decreases to budget authority, entitlement authority, revenues, and public debt subject to statutory limit. It does this by means of a reconciliation bill passed by both Houses of the Congress. The act provides the Congress with a timetable that coordinates the authorization and appropriations cycles with the congressional budget embodied in the concurrent budget resolution. (See below.)

BUDGET ENFORCEMENT AND DEFICIT REDUCTION

Congressional budget enforcement procedures that were established by the Budget Enforcement Act of 1990 (BEA) are designed to reduce or limit the growth in the federal budget deficit each fiscal year through 1995 by establishing yearly "discretionary spending limits," "pay-as-you-go" (PAYGO) requirements for mandatory spending, and "maximum deficit amounts." For discretionary spending, BEA established, for fiscal years 1991 through 1993, caps for three separate categories-defense, international, and domestic. If OMB determines that legislation each year will not meet the deficit target or discretionary spending limits, then the President must issue an order to sequester (reduce or cancel) budget authority. Each year, discretionary spending limits and the maximum deficit amount serve as ceilings to limit expenditures while revenues are expected to grow and bring the deficit closer to the 1995 target level. However, certain adjustments can be made to discretionary spending limits (as explained under the definition for Adjustment to Discretionary Spending Limits). PAYGO requirements that any new mandatory spending and revenue legislation be deficit-neutral were designed to help ensure that legislation shall not increase spending more than revenues.

BEA sets forth three types of sequestrations: discretionary, (PAYGO), and deficit. For discretionary programs, BEA sets budget authority and outlay caps that are enforced through the use of discretionary sequestrations which may occur at different times during the year. A within-session discretionary sequester is to occur if any appropriation enacted before July 1 causes any category (defense, international, or domestic) to exceed the relevant discretionary spending limit (cap) for fiscal years 1992 and 1993. For fiscal years 1994 and 1995 a within session discretionary sequestration will occur if any enacted appropriation causes spending to exceed the total cap for all discretionary spending. The within-session sequestrations become effective in the fiscal years for which the resources were appropriated. If any appropriation enacted after June 30 of the fiscal year in progress causes a cap for that fiscal year to be exceeded, the applicable cap for the following fiscal year (the budget year) is reduced by the amount of the overage. In this case, the reductions are not taken against the year in progress. BEA refers to this process as "look-back." Within 15 calendar days after the Congress adjourns to end a session, an end-of-session discretionary sequestration is to occur if spending for a category (see the definition of Category of Discretionary Spending) exceeds its cap because of appropriations enacted after June 30 for the upcoming[3] fiscal year. The end-of-session reductions also become effective in the fiscal year for which the resources were appropriated.

PAYGO sequestrations relate to revenues and direct spending programs. A PAYGO sequestration of direct spending programs is triggered if legislative changes to revenues or direct spending result in a net deficit increase. The calculation is made once each year concurrently with the end-of-session discretionary sequestration calculation (15 days after adjournment). The size of the sequestration is determined by adding the impact of legislated changes on the current year's deficit to the portion of the preceding year's deficit that was not offset by an earlier sequestration. This "look-back" into the preceding year discourages passage of legislation that increases the deficit after a sequestration report is issued.

A deficit sequestration is triggered if the deficit target for a given year is exceeded by more than a specified margin. The margin for 1992 and 1993 is zero and for 1994 and 1995 is $15 billion. This is a back-up sequestration and is applicable only if an excess deficit greater than the margin remains after any requisite discretionary and PAYGO sequestrations. However, if the discretionary spending limits and the pay-as-you-go requirement for direct spending are met, the maximum deficit amount should not be exceeded through fiscal year 1993. Half of any deficit sequestration must come from defense and half from nondefense programs. Thus, BEA retains the previous Gramm-Rudman-Hollings sequestration process based on deficit targets (although under BEA the deficit targets are adjustable each year).

Budget enforcement procedures require the President to submit a budget consistent with the requirements of the Balanced Budget and Emergency Deficit Control Act. The budget must include estimates of total receipts, total outlays, the deficit, and other aggregate-level estimates using the same estimating rules that are specified for other

---

[3] Technically, an "end-of-session" sequestration may apply to the current fiscal year because Congress may remain in session in October, November, and December. During those months, the "upcoming" fiscal year has become the current fiscal year. To avoid confusion, BEA states that end-of-session sequestration is designed to eliminate "a budget year breach" and defines "budget year" as the fiscal year beginning in "October 1 of the calendar year" in which a congressional session begins. This discussion uses the phrase "the upcoming fiscal year" for simplicity's sake.

reports required by the act. The congressional budget process, including reconciliation, should ensure that the deficit target will be met.

CONGRESSIONAL TIMETABLE

The following timetable lists key steps in the congressional budget process. Two sorts of actions, however, do not fall neatly within the timetable because the times at which they may occur vary considerably.

(1) **Within-session sequestration** applies if the enactment of an appropriation before July 1 causes a "breach," that is, causes a discretionary spending limit to be exceeded. When a breach occurs, CBO must issue to OMB and the Congress a within-session sequestration report within 10 days after the enactment of the appropriation and OMB must issue to the President and the Congress a within-session sequestration report within 15 days after enactment. These reports must contain the amount of the breach, the sequestration percentages necessary to achieve the required reduction, and the amount to be sequestered.

(2) CBO may issue a Low-Growth Report to the Congress at any time that, under standards set by the Budget Enforcement Act (see definition of Low-Growth Report), the economy is in a period of low growth. BEA establishes procedures to suspend sequestration in the event of a Low-Growth Report.

January-February (after the first Monday in January but not later thanthe first Monday in February): Receipt of the President's budget request

Five days before the President submits his budget, the Congressional Budget Office must submit to the Congress a sequestration preview report that contains budget year estimates for the applicable discretionary spending limits for each category, the maximum deficit amount, the excess deficit, the amount of direct spending reductions required, the excess deficit remaining after such reductions have been made, and the amount of reductions required (if a deficit sequestration is predicted) in defense and nondefense accounts.

The Congress begins its budget process when it receives the upcoming fiscal year's executive budget. With the executive budget, the Director of OMB must submit a sequestration preview report setting forth (1) the discretionary spending limits for each fiscal year through 1995, (2) PAYGO data, and (3) deficit sequestration data. The

Congressional Budget Act of 1974, as amended, requires that the President also transmit current services estimates to the Congress. The House and Senate Budget Committees, in preparation for drafting the concurrent resolution on the budget, then hold hearings to examine the President's economic assumptions and spending priorities.

February 15: CBO Submits Report to the Congress

CBO submits to the Budget Committees its annual report on fiscal policy detailing the budgetary impact of alternative revenue levels and spending patterns, including current services spending. This report includes CBO's analysis of the economy and the anticipated impact of the economy on the budget. At the request of the Appropriations Committees, CBO also prepares an analysis of the President's request.

Within 6 weeks of the President's submission of the budget: Committees transmit "views and estimates" to Budget Committees

While the Budget Committees examine aggregate budget levels and budget functions, the other committees (authorization and appropriation) of the Congress transmit to the Budget Committees their "views and estimates" on appropriate spending or revenue levels for programs under their jurisdiction. These views and estimates reports are used by the Budget Committees to gauge the total and functional spending estimates that will be contained in the concurrent budget resolution. In conjunction with these views and estimates reports, the Joint Economic Committee submits its recommendations concerning fiscal policy to the Budget Committees.

March-April: The Congress drafts and passes budget resolution

- **March**: Budget Committees begin drafting budget resolutions.
- **April 1**: Senate Budget Committee reports concurrent resolution on the budget.
- **April 15**: The Congress adopts a budget resolution.

During March, the Budget Committees use the President's budget request, information from their own hearings, views and estimates reports from other committees, and CBO's reports to draft their respective budget resolutions. During this time, the Joint Economic Committee submits its recommendations regarding fiscal policy appropriate to the goals of the Employment Act of 1946 to the House and Senate Budget Committees. Under the Congressional Budget Act of

1974, the Senate Budget Committee is required to report its version of the concurrent resolution on the budget to the full Senate by April 1. The act does not specify dates for action by the House Budget Committee, the full Senate or the full House except that both the House and the Senate must adopt a single compromise budget resolution by April 15. In practice, the Congress has generally passed its budget resolution by May or June. Because the budget resolution is designed solely to guide the Congress in its detailed deliberations on the budget, it is in the form of a concurrent resolution which is agreed to by both houses but not signed by the President.

This resolution establishes the appropriate levels of:

(1) **budget authority,**
(2) **outlays,**
(3) **budget surplus or deficit,**
(4) **federal revenues, and**
(5) **the increase in the debt subject to statutory limit.**

Under budget enforcement procedures, the budget resolution must conform to the same maximum deficit amounts for fiscal years 1992 through 1995 as the President's budget or face a possible point of order on the floor of the House or Senate. The Senate requirement applies to only the first year covered by the budget resolution. Any member of the Congress may raise a point of order against any budget resolution or amendment to a budget resolution that would cause the deficit to exceed those levels. If a budget resolution or amendment to the budget resolution is objected to, it cannot be considered unless applicable House or Senate rules are waived. Waiver of this point of order requires 60 votes in the Senate. In the House, Budget Act points of order are waived by the adoption of "special rules" simple resolutions that provide for the consideration of legislation by the House.

When the Senate and House have both passed their respective versions of the budget resolution, they appoint several of their members to a conference committee to resolve the differences between the two versions. Each chamber must then vote on the compromise version of the resolution, which also must conform to the maximum deficit amounts. The Congressional Budget Act of 1974, as amended, sets April 15 as the date for completion of this work, but no penalty exists for completing the process later. The joint explanatory statement accompanying a conference report on the budget resolution must include an allocation of budget authority and outlays to each committee of the House and Senate with jurisdiction over such authority.

May-September: Spending and revenue bills and reconciliation

- **May 15**: Annual appropriation bills may be considered in the House even if no budget resolution has been adopted.
- **June 10**: House Appropriations Committee reports last annual appropriation bill.
- **June 15**: The Congress completes action on reconciliation legislation.
- **June 30**: The House completes action on annual appropriation bills.
- **July 15**: The Congress receives mid-session review from the President.
- **May-September:** Throughout this period, actions are taken on spending and revenue bills and reconciliation legislation.

After the Congress has adopted a concurrent resolution on the budget, it works on specific spending and revenue measures and on any reconciliation legislation mandated by this budget plan. However, the Congress may pass appropriations bills after May 15 without having passed a budget resolution, but appropriations bills whose amounts are not consistent with maximum deficit amount established by BEA are subject to a point of order. (See definitions of Maximum Deficit Amount and Point of Order.) Under the congressional budget timetable, the House Appropriations Committee should report its last annual appropriation bill by June 10 and the Congress should complete action on reconciliation legislation by June 15. Action on annual appropriation bills is to be completed in the House by June 30 and in the Senate by the start of the fiscal year (October 1). Action on appropriations bills has not always been completed by October 1, necessitating the passage of a continuing resolution to provide authority to continue financing agency operations up to a specific date or until a regular appropriation is enacted.

During spring and summer, as the Congress works on spending and revenue measures and reconciliation legislation for the upcoming fiscal year, the levels set in the budget resolution stand as constraints on congressional actions. CBO tabulates a report on new spending authority and new budget authority and transmits the updated report to the Budget Committees at least once a month. In the Senate, to enforce the limitations in the budget resolution, any Senator can object to legislation that would violate the spending ceiling or revenue floor or that would cause the maximum deficit amount for that year to be exceeded. House rules also generally prohibit exceeding the budget resolution totals, and, in both bodies, spending allocations are enforced by points of order, although in different ways.

If changing economic circumstances or policy requirements dictate, the Congress may revise its budget resolution during the fiscal year, thereby altering the spending and revenue totals. However, it is not in order in the Senate to consider any bill, resolution, amendment, motion, or conference report that would violate the maximum deficit amount. One example of new information that the Congress receives which could cause it to revise its budget resolution is the President's mid-session review of the budget, issued on July 15.

August 15-20: CBO's and OMB's deficit estimates and initial reports

- **August 15**: CBO issues its sequestration update report to OMB and the Congress.
- **August 20**: OMB issues its sequestration update report to the President and the Congress.

On August 15, CBO issues its sequestration update report, which comprises a discretionary sequestration report, a PAYGO sequestration report, and a deficit sequestration report. The discretionary sequestration report sets forth the discretionary spending limits for the current fiscal year and each subsequent year through 1995 and an explanation of any adjustments in the limits. The PAYGO sequestration report sets forth (1) the net deficit increase or decrease due to direct spending, (2) a list identifying each enacted law and implemented sequestration (after the date of enactment of the Budget Enforcement Act) included in calculating the amount of deficit increase or decrease and specifying the budgetary effect of each such law, and (3) the percent of sequestrable direct spending that must be sequestered to eliminate a deficit increase. The deficit sequestration report contains the maximum deficit amount, the estimated deficit, the excess deficit, the margin, the amount of required PAYGO reductions, the excess deficit remaining after those reductions have been made, and the sequestration percent necessary to achieve the required reductions in defense and nondefense accounts. OMB's sequestration update report contains the same type of information.

October 1: Fiscal year begins

The new fiscal year begins October 1 and extends through September 30 of the following year. If action on appropriations is not completed when the fiscal year starts, the Congress may enact a continuing resolution. After the President signs this resolution or allows it to become law without his signature, it gives agencies authority to continue operations, pending the possible enactment of regular appropriations.

After the end of the annual congressional session:
CBO and OMB issue their final sequestration reports
and GAO issues compliance report

The Congress ends its annual session on varying dates but the end of session almost always occurs between August and January. Under the Budget Enforcement Act, certain actions must occur following the end of a congressional session.

- **10 days after the end of session**, CBO issues its final sequestration report.
- **15 days after the end of session**, OMB issues its final sequestration report and the President, if necessary, issues an order to implement all sequestrations required by the calculations in OMB's report.
- **30 days after the submission of OMB's report**, GAO issues its compliance report.

CBO's final sequestration report contains essentially the same types of information, brought up to date, contained in its preview report (issued 5 days before the President's budget) and sequestration update report (issued by August 15). This report contains a PAYGO and, if necessary, a deficit sequestration report. OMB's final sequestration report explains any differences between OMB and CBO in the estimates of the net deficit change, excess deficit, any breach, and any required sequestration percentage. Similarly, OMB's final sequestration report contains PAYGO and discretionary spending sequestration reports and, if necessary, a deficit sequestration report. The President's order must implement without change the sequestrations required by OMB's report. GAO's report states the extent to which orders issued by the President and reports issued by OMB or CBO comply with applicable Budget Enforcement Act requirements.

PHASE 3: BUDGET EXECUTION AND CONTROL

After the Congress and President enact legislation to create budget authority (subsequently modified by sequestration if necessary) the President is responsible for executing it. OMB regulates the apportionment (distribution) of budget authority granted to the agencies of the executive branch, except for those exempted by law or regulation. The Director of OMB apportions budget authority to each agency by time periods (usually quarters) or by activities over the duration of the appropriation to ensure the economical and effective use of funds and preclude the need for additional appropriations. Changes in law or economic conditions during the fiscal year may necessitate the enactment of additional budget authority. When this happens, supplemental requests are sent to the Congress for its consideration.

The Impoundment Control Act of 1974 permits the President, when proposing rescissions, to initially withhold (that is, delay the obligation of) appropriated funds for fiscal, policy, or other reasons, or because the President has determined that all or part of an appropriation is not needed to carry out a program. Upon making a determination that budget authority is not needed, the President sends a special message to the Congress requesting that the budget authority be rescinded. If the Congress does not pass a rescission bill within 45 legislative days of continuous session, the budget authority is required to be made available for obligation. If the requisite legislation is enacted, the budget authority is rescinded and becomes unavailable for obligation.

Under the Impoundment Control Act of 1974, as amended, the President, the Director of OMB, or an agency or other federal government official may defer and temporarily withhold—budget authority only to provide for contingencies (the President may establish reserves for contingencies), to achieve savings made possible by or through changes in requirements or greater efficiency of operations, or as specifically provided by law (2 U.S.C. 684). Whenever a deferral is proposed, the President must transmit a special message to the Congress explaining the deferral. A deferral remains in effect unless the Congress disapproves it by law. A deferral, however, may not extend beyond the fiscal year in which it was proposed. Nevertheless, in the case of no-year or multiyear budget authority, if continued deferral is desired into the new fiscal year, the President must transmit a new special message to the Congress. Apportionments do not constitute deferrals as long as they are used in a manner consistent with the law (that is, to allow obligation of the full amount appropriated, but to prevent over obligations).

PHASE 4: AUDIT AND EVALUATION

Individual agencies are responsible—through their own review and control systems—for making sure that the obligations they incur and the resulting outlays adhere to the provisions in the authorizing and appropriations legislation as well as to other laws and regulations governing the obligation and expenditure of funds. The Inspector

General Act of 1978, as amended, established agency inspectors general to provide policy direction for and to conduct, supervise, and coordinate audits and investigations relating to agency programs and operations. Also, the Chief Financial Officers Act of 1990 established agency chief financial officers to oversee all financial management activities relating to agency programs and operations. OMB exercises its review responsibility by appraising program and financial reports and by keeping abreast of agencies' efforts to attain program objectives.

In addition, the General Accounting Office (GAO), as an agency responsible to the Congress, regularly audits, examines, and evaluates government programs. Its findings and recommendations for corrective action are made to the Congress, to OMB, and to the agencies concerned. GAO also monitors the executive branch's reporting of messages on deferrals, proposed rescissions, the President's requests to cancel budget authority, and the President's requests to temporarily withhold funds. Should the President fail to make budget authority available in accordance with applicable law, GAO may bring civil action to obtain compliance.

BUDGET FUNCTIONAL CLASSIFICATION

The functional classification system is a way of grouping budgetary resources so that all budget authority and outlays of on-budget and off-budget federal entities and tax expenditures can be presented according to the national needs being addressed. National needs are grouped in 17 broad areas to provide a coherent and comprehensive basis for analyzing and understanding the budget. Three additional categories—Net Interest, Allowances, and Undistributed Offsetting Receipts—do not address specific national needs but are included to cover the entire budget.

To the extent feasible, functional classifications are made without regard to agency or organizational distinctions. Each federal activity is placed in a functional classification that best defines the activity's most important purpose even though many activities serve more than one purpose. This is necessary so that the sum of the functional categories equals the budget totals. The functional classifications are also the categories that the Congress uses in the concurrent resolutions on the budget, pursuant to the Congressional Budget and Impoundment Control Act of 1974 (2 U.S.C. 632). Different programs within a single function may fall under the jurisdiction of different committees.

A function may be divided into two or more subfunctions, depending upon the complexity of the national need addressed by that function. A three-digit code represents each functional subfunctional category. The functional codes also make up the last three digits of the account identification code.

The functional structure is relatively stable, but changes are made from time to time to take into account changing conditions and requirements. As a rule, any changes in this structure are made after OMB consults with the Appropriations and Budget Committees of the Senate and House of Representatives and the Congressional Budget Office.

The following outline of the functional classification structure is taken from the *Budget of the United States Government, Fiscal Year 1993.* The definitions for the subfunctional structure are from the Office of Management and Budget technical staff paper, "The Functional Classification in the Budget" (1979 Revision), Executive Office of The President, OMB, February 22, 1979, Technical Paper Series BRD/FAB 79-1. Where necessary, these definitions have been updated to accommodate changes since issuance of that document. The three digit numbers listed under "Code" and the associated titles and definitions are for the major functions. The three digit numbers listed under "Subcode" and the associated titles and definitions are for the subfunctions.

FUNCTIONAL CLASSIFICATION STRUCTURE

NATIONAL DEFENSE - CODE 050

Common defense and security of the United States. This encompasses the:

- raising, equipping, and maintaining of armed forces (including civilian support activities), development and utilization of weapons systems (including nuclear weapons), and related programs;
- direct compensation and benefits paid to active military and civilian personnel; contributions to their retirement, health, and life insurance funds;[4]
- defense research, development, testing, and evaluation; and
- procurement, construction, stockpiling, and other activities undertaken to directly foster national security.

Excluded from national defense are

- benefits or compensation to veterans and their dependents and military and civil service retirees
- the peaceful conduct of foreign relations;
- foreign military, economic, and humanitarian assistance;
- subsidies to business by civilian agencies (such as maritime subsidies) that may be partially justified as promoting national security; and

---

[4] For years prior to 1985 when the military retirement trust fund began, the historical data included imputed accruals for retirement, with a matching imputed undistributed offsetting collection (subfunction 951). The cash retirement benefits for all years are included in the income security function.

- research and operations of agencies (such as space research) whose program missions are not directly designed to promote national defense but which could result in some significant benefits to our national security.

Department of Defense-Military - Subcode 051

The entire agency is included in this subfunction.

Atomic energy defense activities - Subcode 053

Department of Energy programs devoted to national defense, such as naval ship reactors and nuclear weapons.

Defense-related activities - Subcode 054

Miscellaneous defense activities, such as the expenses connected with selective services and with defense stockpiles outside of the Departments of Defense and Energy.

INTERNATIONAL AFFAIRS - CODE 150

Maintaining peaceful relations, commerce, and travel between the United States and the rest of the world and promoting international security and economic development abroad. (Excluded are outlays from domestic programs that may tangentially affect foreign relations or the citizens of other nations.)

International development and humanitarian assistance - Subcode151

Humanitarian assistance, development assistance, security support assistance, grants to and investments in international financial and development institutions, and the budgetary costs associated with concessionary agricultural exports.

International security assistance - Subcode 152

The transfer of defense articles and services to foreign governments, including grants, credit sales, and training. Excluded is the military sales trust fund, which is classified under subfunction 155 (international financial programs).

Conduct of foreign affairs - Subcode 153

Diplomatic and consular operations of the Department of State, assessed contributions to international organizations, and closely related activities in other agencies (such as the Arms Control and Disarmament Agency).

Foreign information and exchange activities - Subcode 154

Student and cultural exchange programs and foreign library, radio, or other media information activities designed to promote mutual understanding between the people of the United States and other nations.

International financial programs - Subcode 155

Export credit, the military sales trust fund, international commodity agreements, international monetary programs, and other programs designed to improve the functioning of the international financial system. For pre-1992 credit programs, includes the total cost of loans and the cost of honoring loan guarantees. For loans or loan guarantees obligated or committed after 1991, includes the credit subsidy cost of the loans or guarantees.

GENERAL SCIENCE, SPACE, AND TECHNOLOGY - CODE 250

Budget resources allocated to science and research activities of the federal government that are not an integral part of the programs conducted under any other function. This function includes the research conducted by the National Science Foundation, all space programs conducted by the National Aeronautics and Space Administration, and general science research supported by the Department of Energy. Research and technology programs that have diverse goals and cannot readily be classified under one specific function are also placed here to avoid detailed splitting of accounts.

General science and basic research - Subcode 251

Conducting the National Science Foundation programs and the general science activities of the Department of Energy.

Space flight, research, and supporting activities - Subcode 252

Development and operation of space transportation systems, basic scientific research connected with outer space, research and demonstrations designed to promote terrestrial applications of technology developed through space research, and development of new space technologies for future flight missions. Also included are costs of tracking and data relay support for the National Aeronautics and Space Administration space science and applications for flight missions.

ENERGY - CODE 270

Promoting an adequate supply and appropriate use of energy to serve the needs of the economy. Included are the energy programs of the Department of Energy and its predecessor agencies. Excluded are atomic energy defense activities and general science research not closely related to energy.

Energy supply - Subcode 271

Increasing the supply of energy through the development of domestic resources and systems capable of using them. Includes the costs of research and demonstration of supply systems.

Energy conservation - Subcode 271

Encouraging the prudent use of energy resources.

Emergency energy preparedness - Subcode 274

Developing and maintaining a stockpile of energy resources (currently confined to petroleum) to meet emergency needs and associated contingency planning activities.

Energy information, policy, and regulation - Subcode 276

Unallocable overhead activities of the Department of Energy plus the costs of energy information and regulation activities.

NATURAL RESOURCES AND ENVIRONMENT - CODE 300

Developing, managing, and maintaining the nation's natural resources and environment. Excluded are the outlays for community water supply programs, basic sewer systems, and waste treatment plants, all of which are part of a community or regional development (rather than an environmental enhancement) program or are part of the cost of operating a federal facility (such as a military installation).

Water resources - Subcode 301

Water protection, conservation, irrigation, and related activities, including the total costs of multipurpose water projects where it is not feasible to separate the transportation (navigation) or energy (power) segments of these projects.

Conservation and land management - Subcode 302

Maintaining the public domain and national forests, encouraging conservation of private land, and reclaiming surface mining areas.

Recreational resources - Subcode 303

Acquisition, improvement, and operation of recreational lands and facilities, including fish, wildlife, and parks; also preserving historic areas.

Pollution control and abatement - Subcode 304

Controlling and reducing air, water, and land pollution, or enhancing the environment. Excluded are water resources programs, water treatment plants, and similar programs that are not funded as part of an environmental enhancement activity.

Other natural resources - Subcode 306

Miscellaneous natural resources programs, not classified under other subfunctions, such as marine, earth, and atmosphere-related research, and geological surveys and mapping.

AGRICULTURE - CODE 350

Promoting the economic stability of agriculture and the nation's capability to maintain and increase agricultural production. Excluded are programs which, though related to rural development, are not directly related to agriculture, such as rural environmental and conservation programs classified in the natural resources function. Also excluded are concessionary food export sales or food donations, whether overseas or for domestic income support purposes.

Farm income stabilization - Subcode 351

Subsidies and other payments to stabilize agricultural prices at an equitable level. This subfunction includes acquiring and storing agricultural commodity stock piles but does not include foreign agricultural export losses (classified in the international affairs function) or domestic donations of food (part of an income support, rather than a farm price support, program). Farm price support loans (that is, loans that can be repaid in cash or by surrendering title to the crop used as security for the loan) are excluded from credit reform (and, thus, are retained on-budget on a cash basis). All other agricultural loans and loan guarantees are included in credit reform, so only the credit subsidy cost of the credit is included in the budget.

Agricultural research and services - Subcode 352

All other agricultural programs, such as agricultural research and extension services.

COMMERCE AND HOUSING CREDIT - CODE 370

Promotion and regulation of commerce and the housing credit and deposit insurance industries, which pertain to

- collection and dissemination of social and economic data (unless they are an integral part of another function, such as health),
- general purpose subsidies to business, including credit subsidies to the housing industry. For credit programs under credit reform, only the credit subsidy cost of loans and loan guarantees are included; and
- the Postal Service fund and general fund subsidies of that fund.

In general, credit and insurance programs are included in this function; however, if such programs are a means of achieving the basic objectives of another function and are an integral part of the programs of that function, they are classified under the other function.

Excluded are regional economic development programs, even if they use credit or insurance to achieve a community development objective. Also excluded are other insurance or loan programs (such as railroad loans) that are an integral part of other functions.

Mortgage credit - Subcode 371

Includes the cash transactions for homeownership and related loan and insurance programs for pre-credit reform activity; under credit reform, includes the credit subsidy cost of any homeownership loans or guarantees.

Postal service - Subcode 372

Any net outlays of the Postal Service included in the budget (or off-budget).

Deposit insurance - Subcode 373

Insurance programs protecting deposits in certain financial institutions; programs to resolve failed institutions. Deposit insurance activities are not included under credit reform, so the budget records the cash flows for deposit insurance rather than their subsidy values.

Other advancement of commerce - Subcode 376

Loan programs to aid specialized forms of business (such as small business) that are not included elsewhere in the functional structure. For such transactions undertaken prior to credit reform, includes the total cash flows. For activities under credit reform, includes the credit subsidy cost of the loans or guarantees. Also included are collecting and disseminating economic and demographic statistics (such as census data) and regulating business.

TRANSPORTATION - CODE 400

Providing for the transportation of the general public and/or its property, regardless of whether local or national and regardless of the particular mode of transportation. This classification includes

- construction of facilities;
- purchase of equipment;
- research, testing, and evaluation;
- provision of communications directly related to transportation (for example, air traffic control by the Federal Aviation Administration);
- operating subsidies for transportation facilities (such as airports) and industries (such as railroads); and
- regulatory activities directed specifically toward the transportation industry rather than toward business.

Excluded are

- moving personnel or equipment as part of the operation of other government services;
- foreign economic assistance that may involve assisting transportation facilities or programs abroad;
- the construction of roads or trails as an integral part of the operation of public lands, parks, forests, or military reservations, unless they are specifically funded as a part of a broader transportation program;
- the construction of roads or other transportation facilities as an integral part of a broad community facility or regional development program where the clear intent of the program is regional development and the provision of transportation facilities is only an incidental by-product or means to attain the objective of regional development; and
- research and technology activities devoted to space research (except aeronautical technology), even though this research may eventually benefit general transportation.

Ground transportation - Subcode 401

Aid for and/or regulation of the various components of ground transportation, such as roads and highways, railroads, and urban mass transit.

Air transportation - Subcode 402

Aid for and/or regulation of air transportation, including aeronautical research conducted by NASA.

Water transportation - Subcode 403

Aid for and/or regulation of maritime commerce.

Other transportation - Subcode 407

General transportation programs and overhead not readily allocable to any of the preceding subfunctions.

COMMUNITY AND REGIONAL DEVELOPMENT - CODE 450

Development of physical facilities or financial infrastructures designed to promote viable community economies. Transportation facilities developed as an integral part of a community development program (rather than a transportation program) are also included. Aids to businesses are not usually included in this function unless such aids promote the economic development of depressed areas and are not designed to promote particular lines of business for their own sake. Human development and services programs are usually excluded from this function.

Community development - Subcode 451

Grants and related programs designed to aid largely urban community development. Included are community development block grants and predecessor activities such as the urban renewal and model cities programs. These programs are generally carried out by the Department of Housing and Urban Development.

Area and regional development - Subcode 452

Grants, loans, subsidies, and related aids for the economic development of depressed areas. For precredit reform loans, includes the cash flows of the loans; for loans under credit reform, includes the credit subsidy cost of the loans. All these aids are generally for rural areas or are more regional than the community development programs. Area and regional development programs are generally carried out by agencies other than the Department of Housing and Urban Development, such as the Farmers Home Administration, Economic Development Administration, and Bureau of Indian Affairs.

Disaster relief and insurance - Subcode 453

Helping communities and families recover from natural disasters.

EDUCATION, TRAINING, EMPLOYMENT, AND SOCIAL SERVICES - CODE 500

Promoting the extension of knowledge and skills, enhancing employment and employment opportunities, protecting workplace standards, and providing services to the needy. This function excludes education or training undertaken as an integral part of the achievement of other functions (such as training military personnel; veterans education, training, and rehabilitation; or training of health workers in a health program). Nutrition or food service programs funded separately from social services or education are not part of this function--they are classified as income security.

Elementary, secondary, and vocational education - Code 501

Preschool, elementary, secondary, and vocational education programs.

Higher education - Subcode 502

College and graduate school programs.

Research and general education aids - Subcode 503

Education research and assistance for the arts, the humanities, educational radio and television, public libraries, and museums.

Training and employment - Subcode 504

Job or skill training, employment services and placement, and payments to employers to subsidize employment.

Other labor services - Subcode 505

Aids to or regulation of the labor market, including gathering labor statistics and mediation and conciliation services; excludes other than employment and training programs, and occupational safety and health programs.

Social services - Subcode 506

Programs that provide a broad range of services to individuals to help them improve their vocational capabilities (such as vocational rehabilitation) or family status; services to the poor and elderly that are not primarily for income support and that are not an integral part of some other function (such as social service block grants).

HEALTH -CODE 550

Programs other than medicare whose basic purpose is to promote physical and mental health, including the prevention of illness and accidents. The medicare program is the largest federal health program, but by law it is in a separate function (function 570). Also excluded from the health function is federal health care for military personnel (051) and veterans (703). General scientific research that has medical applications (such as that conducted by the National Science Foundation) and health programs financed through foreign assistance programs are also excluded.

Health care services - Subcode 551

Providing medical services to individuals and families, whether such services are provided directly by the federal government or financed through grants, contracts, insurance, or reimbursements.

Health research and training - Subcode 552

All research programs-whether basic or applied--that are financed specifically as health or medical research. Excludes research that is an integral part of other functions (such as biomedical research in the space program). Also includes any education or training program specifically funded as a health program and restricted to training individuals who work, or expect to work, in health or health-related fields.

Consumer and occupational health and safety - Subcode 554

Meat and poultry inspection, food and drug inspection, consumer product safety, and occupational health and safety.

MEDICARE - CODE 570

Federal hospital insurance and federal supplementary medical insurance, along with general fund subsidies of these funds and associated offsetting receipts.

Medicare - Subcode 571

Entire medicare function.

INCOME SECURITY - CODE 600

Support payments (including associated administrative expenses) to persons for whom no current service is rendered. Included are retirement, disability, unemployment, welfare, and similar programs, except for social security and income security for veterans, which are in other functions. Also included are the food stamp, special milk, and child nutrition programs (whether the benefits are in cash or in kind); both federal and trust fund unemployment compensation and workers' compensation; public assistance cash payments; benefits to the elderly and to coal miners; and low- and moderate-income housing benefits.

Excluded are (a) financial assistance for education, (b) medical care (whether in cash or in kind), (c) subsidies to business (such as farm price supports), and (d) reimbursement for child care services, even though any of these may end up as income to persons. Also excluded are income security programs included in the social security function (function 650) and programs restricted to veterans and their dependents.

General retirement and disability insurance - (excluding social security) - Subcode 601

Non-needs-tested retirement and disability programs composed mainly of the railroad retirement fund and special benefits for coal miners. Excluded are programs specifically restricted to federal employees.

Federal employee retirement and disability - Subcode 602

All funded retirement and disability programs restricted to federal employees. Military retirement benefits are included in this function for all years, not just the years since the military retirement program began as a funded trust fund (1985). In cases where retirement benefits are not funded (such as in the case of Coast Guard retired pay), the cash benefits are included in the function where the employees were employed (in the Coast Guard case, transportation), because otherwise those functions would never be charged for the retirement costs of their employees.

Unemployment compensation - Subcode 603

Benefits not conditioned by needs tests for unemployed workers. Excluded are other benefits (such as food stamps) that an unemployed person might be eligible for under other programs.

Housing assistance - Subcode 604

Federal income support and related expenses that are specifically for financing or providing housing for individuals and families. Excluded are loans, loan guarantees, or insurance. (The distinction between the housing assistance included in subfunction 604 and the mortgage credit assistance in subfunction 371 is that the subfunction 604 payments focus on subsidies to increase beneficiaries' effective income, whereas the credit subsidies in subfunction 371 are primarily aimed at encouraging the housing industry.)

Food and nutrition assistance - Subcode 605

Providing food or nutritional assistance to individuals and families.

Other income security - Subcode 609

Income security programs not included in any other subfunction. Primarily either direct payments or grants-in-aid to finance direct payments that constitute cash income to low-income individuals and families. Also includes refugee assistance and both administrative expenses and offsetting collections in the income security function that are not part of any other subfunction.

SOCIAL SECURITY - CODE 650

Federal old age and survivors and disability insurance trust funds, along with general fund subsidies of these funds and associated offsetting collections.

Social security - Subcode 651

The entire social security function is included in one subfunction.

VETERANS BENEFITS AND SERVICES - CODE 700

Programs providing benefits and services, the eligibility for which is related to prior military service, but the financing of which is not an integral part of the costs of national defense. As a rule, the outlays in this function are similar to those in the broader general purpose functions (such as income security or health), but are restricted to veterans, their dependents, and their survivors. Earned rights of career military personnel that are a cost of the defense budget (such as military retired pay or medical care) are excluded.

Income security for veterans - Subcode 701

Veterans' compensation, life insurance, pensions, and burial benefits.

Veterans education, training, and rehabilitation - Subcode 702

Composed primarily of the "GI bill" readjustment, vocational rehabilitation benefits, and related programs.

Hospital and medical care for veterans - Subcode 703

Medical care and research financed by the Department of Veterans Affairs.

Veterans housing - Subcode 704

Housing loan and guarantee programs for veterans and dependents. Pre-1992 housing loans and guarantees are recorded on a cash basis, whereas under credit reform (post-1991), the budget records the credit subsidy cost of the activity.

Other veterans benefits and services - Subcode 705

Administrative expenses of the Department of Veterans Affairs.

ADMINISTRATION OF JUSTICE - CODE 750

Programs to provide judicial services, police protection, law enforcement (including civil rights), rehabilitation and incarceration of criminals, and the general maintenance of domestic order. It includes the provision of court appointed counsel or other legal services for individuals. It excludes the cost of the legislative branch, the police or guard activities to protect federal property, and activities that are an integral part of a broader function (such as postal inspectors, tax collection agents, and Park Service Rangers). The cost of National Guard personnel and military personnel who are called upon occasionally to maintain public safety and the cost of military police are included under the national defense function rather than this function.

Federal law enforcement activities - Subcode 751

The costs of operating the Federal Bureau of Investigation, the United States Customs Service, the Immigration and Naturalization Service, the Drug Enforcement Administration, and police and crime prevention activities in other programs. Also includes the readily identifiable enforcement cost of civil rights activities.

Federal litigative and judicial activities - Subcode 752

The cost of the judiciary, the cost of prosecution, and federal expenses connected with financing legal defense activities.

Federal correctional activities - Subcode 753

Covers the costs of incarceration, supervision, parole, and rehabilitation of federal prisoners.

Criminal justice assistance - Subcode 754

Grants to state and local governments to assist them in operating and improving their law enforcement and justice systems.

GENERAL GOVERNMENT - CODE 800

General overhead costs of the federal government, including legislative and executive activities; provision of central fiscal, personnel, and property activities; provision of services that cannot reasonably be classified in any other major function. As a rule, all activities reasonably or closely associated with other functions are included in those functions rather than being listed as part of general government. Also includes shared revenues and other general purpose fiscal assistance.

Legislative functions - Subcode 801

Includes most of the legislative branch. However, the Library of Congress (except the Congressional Research Service), the Tax Court, the Government Printing Office (except for congressional printing and binding), and the Copyright Royalty Tribunal are classified in other subfunctions.

Executive direction and management - Subcode 802

The Executive Office of the President (unless some major grants or operating programs should be included in the Office); occasionally some closely related spending outside the Office is included.

Central fiscal operations - Subcode 803

Covers the general tax collection and fiscal operations of the Department of the Treasury.

General property and records management - Subcode 804

Most of the operations of the General Services Administration (net of reimbursements from other agencies for services rendered).

Central personnel management - Subcode 805

Most of the operating costs of the Office of Personnel Management and related agencies (net of reimbursements from other agencies for services rendered).

General purpose fiscal assistance - Subcode 806

Federal aid to state, local, and territorial governments that is available for general fiscal support. The transactions of the now discontinued general revenue sharing program are included in the historical data for this subfunction. Also included in this subfunction are grants for more restricted purposes when the stipulated purposes cross two or more major budgetary functions and the distribution among those functions is at the discretion of the recipient jurisdiction rather than the federal government. It includes payments in lieu of taxes, broad purpose shared revenues, and the federal payments to the District of Columbia. Payments specifically for community development or social services programs are not included in this function.

Other general government - Subcode 808

Miscellaneous other costs, such as federal costs of territorial governments.

Deductions for offsetting receipts - Subcode 809

Includes general government function offsetting receipts that are not closely related to any other subfunction in this function.

NET INTEREST - CODE 900

Transactions which directly give rise to interest payments or income (lending) and the general shortfall or excess of outgoing over income arising out of fiscal, monetary, and other policy considerations and leading to the creation of interest-bearing debt instruments (normally the public debt). The net interest function includes interest paid on the public debt, on uninvested funds, and on tax refunds, offset by interest collections.

Interest on the public debt - Subcode 901

Outlays for interest on the public debt. (Where this interest is paid to the public, it is on an accrual basis; all other interest outlays in the budget are on a cash basis.)

Interest received by on-budget trust funds - Subcode 902

Interfund interest collected by on-budget nonrevolving trust funds. Most of this income derives from outlays included in subfunction 901, but this subfunction also includes offsetting receipts from investments in public debt securities issued by the Federal Financing Bank.

Interest received by off-budget trust funds - Subcode 903

Interfund interest collected by off-budget nonrevolving trust funds. Normally all of this income comes from outlays included in subfunction 901.

Other interest - Subcode 908

All other interest expenditures and offsetting receipts. The principal expenditure in this subfunction normally is interest on refunds of receipts. Since offsetting interest receipts are included in this subfunction, the subfunction totals are usually negative.

Allowances - Subcode 920

The budget always includes estimates for allowances for future years. Since the Congress never appropriates money for "allowances" but only specific programs, there are never any budget authority or outlay totals for allowances in any past periods. However, this category is needed to permit the budget to reflect the total estimated budget authority and outlay requirements for future years.

In addition to the budget authority and outlays in each of the functional classifications, the President's budget normally includes some budget authority and outlays classified as allowances. The allowance categories in the budget follow.

Contingencies for specific requirements - Subcode 922-929

The specific line entries will vary from budget to budget, depending on what projections are required.

UNDISTRIBUTED OFFSETTING RECEIPTS - CODE 950

Most offsetting receipts are included as deductions from outlays in the applicable functions and subfunctions. However, there are five major categories of offsetting receipts that are classified as undistributed offsetting receipts rather than being included as an offset in any of the other functions.

Employer share, employee retirement (on-budget) - Subcode 951

Employing agency payments to funded retirement systems of federal employees are intragovernmental transactions (that is, they are payments by government accounts collected by other government accounts) and, hence, both the payment and collection are included in federal outlays. The payments are included in the various agency outlays, while the offsets are undistributed.[5]

Most federal employees are now covered by the hospital insurance portion of the medicare program. The employing agency payments to the hospital insurance fund are also offset in this subfunction.

Employer share, employee retirement (off-budget)- Subcode 952

This category includes collections similar in nature to those in subfunction 951, except that the accounts collecting the money are off-budget.

Rents and royalties on the outer continental shelf - Subcode 953

Rents and royalties on the outer continental shelf constitute a large source of nontax income that is largely a windfall to the government. Since there are no major government programs that give rise to this income, it would be inappropriate to offset it against the outlays in any function. Thus, the collections are undistributed.

Sale of major assets - Subcode 954

On occasion, the government derives large returns from the sale of major assets, and the proceeds of the sales are recorded in this category rather than in any major function.

---

[5] The historical data for this category for years prior to 1985 include an offset equal to the imputed accrual for military retirement that is included in subfunction 051. These imputations were calculated so that the data for the years prior to the creation of the military retirement trust fund would be as comparable as feasible with the subsequent years.

Other undistributed offsetting receipts - Subcode 959

This category includes items such as collections for the lease of federal lands for petroleum exploitation and a proposal for the Federal Communications Commission to conduct auctions.

FEDERAL BUDGET ACCOUNT
IDENTIFICATION CODE

Each account, or group of accounts, in the federal budget is assigned an 11-digit identification code by OMB in coordination with the Department of the Treasury. Each identification code is printed in the program and financing schedules, schedules on direct and guaranteed loans, and object class schedules of the "Detailed Budget Estimates" section of the federal budget.

FEDERAL BUDGET ACCOUNT IDENTIFICATION CODES

Digits	Explanation
XX-xxxx-x-x-xxx	The first two digits designate the *agency code* assigned by the Department of the Treasury.
xx-XXXX-x-x-xxx	The third through sixth digits designate the *appropriation or fund account symbol* assigned by Treasury. When two or more accounts with different Treasury basic account symbols are included in a consolidated schedule, "99" is used for the third and fourth digits. The fifth digit is the fund type. (See eighth digit description below.) The sixth digit reflects the sequence in which the consolidated accounts for a particular agency appear in the budget.
xx-xxxx-X-x-xxx	The seventh digit designates the *transmittal code* which identifies the nature or timing of the transmittal of the estimates, as follows:

0 = Regular budget schedule
1 = Supplemental under existing legislation

2 = Proposed for later transmittal under proposed legislation
3 = Proposed for later transmittal under existing legislation
4 = Supplemental—additional authorizing legislation required
5 = Rescission proposal
7 = Legislative action required

xx-xxxx-x-X-xxx   The eighth digit identifies the *type of fund,* as follows:

1 = General fund
2 = Special fund
3 = Public enterprise fund
4 = Intragovernmental revolving or management fund
7 = Trust (nonrevolving) fund
8 = Trust revolving fund

xx-xxxx-x-x-XXX   The last three digits designate **functional** *classification as* used in the latest budget documents, unless otherwise noted by OMB. Where a schedule is split between two or more subfunctions, the following apply: (1) If all subfunctions are in the same major function, the code of the major function is used. (2) If two or more major functions are involved, "999" is used.

An alternate 13-digit identification code is also used by OMB to generate certain tables and summaries in the budget. This code substitutes a four-digit OMB agency/bureau code assigned by OMB for the two-digit agency code assigned by the Department of the Treasury. The alternate OMB code was developed because the Treasury coding embeds agency codes in such a way that they cannot be used for sequencing by agency. The first two digits of the OMB code[6] represent an agency identification code; the third and fourth digits represent a subordinate unit within the agency, such as a bureau. The remaining nine digits of the account code are identical.

---

[6] OMB agency codes are not the same as Treasury agency codes.

PROGRAM AND FINANCING SCHEDULE

This schedule consists of three parts. In the "Program by activities" section, obligations generally are shown for specific activities or projects. To provide a meaningful presentation of information for the program being financed, the activity structure is developed individually for each appropriation or fund account. That structure is tailored to the individual account and is not uniform across the government. When the amounts of obligations that are financed from collections credited to an account (reimbursements) are significant, "reimbursable program" obligations are shown separately from "direct program" obligations. When the amounts are significant, "capital investments" are shown separately from "operating expenses." The last entry, "total obligations," indicates the minimum amount of budgetary resources that must be available to the appropriation or fund account in that year.

The "Financing" section shows the total budgetary resources available or estimated to be available to finance the total obligations. This section lists (1) the unobligated balances of budgetary resources (that have not expired) brought forward from the end of the prior year, and (2) those amounts that were available for obligation during the year and were not used, but continue to be available, are shown as an unobligated balance available, end of year. That balance is carried forward and usually obligated in a subsequent year. Other adjusting entries may be included. The residual is the new budget authority required to finance the program. Where more than one kind of budget authority is provided, that information is shown. In some cases, the availability of budgetary resources may be restrained by legally binding limitations on obligations. Such limitations are usually included in appropriations language.

The "Relation of obligations to outlays" section shows the difference between obligations, which may not be liquidated in the same year in which they are incurred, and outlays. The entry "total obligations" shows the amount of new obligations incurred in the year. The amount of obligations that were incurred in previous years but not liquidated are entered as an obligated balance start of year. Similarly, an end of year obligated balance is entered. Certain adjusting entries may be included. The residual is the total amount of outlays resulting from the liquidation of obligations incurred in that year and previous years.

The "Adjustments to budget authority and outlays" section shows deductions for offsetting collections for those accounts that are credited with such collections. The amounts are listed by source— federal funds, trust funds, non-federal sources, or off-budget federal accounts. The total amount of collections is deducted from gross budget authority and gross outlays. The residual is net budget authority and net outlays. For accounts with limitations on the authority to spend offsetting collections, the balance of any amount that is unavailable for obligation is shown at the bottom of the schedule.

An 11-digit identification code, found at the top of the program and financing schedule, facilitates computer processing of budgetary information. The Program and Financing Schedule is preceded by the language of the appropriation acts (fiscal year 1992 in the following sample) and is printed following the account title. The language of the previous year's appropriation act is used as a base. Brackets enclose material proposed for deletion; italic type indicates proposed language. When an appropriation has not been enacted at the time the budget is submitted, the language relates only to the fiscal year in question and is italicized, with no brackets shown. In a few cases, the language from unenacted appropriation bills is used as a base. In such cases, the language is followed by an explanatory note.

At the end of the final appropriation language paragraph, and printed in italics within parentheses, are citations to relevant authorizing legislation and to the appropriation act from which the basic text of the language is taken.

EXAMPLE OF PROGRAM AND FINANCING SCHEDULE PRECEDED BY APPROPRIATIONS LANGUAGE (EXECUTIVE BUDGET) FOR U.S. DEPARTMENT OF AGRICULTURE PROGRAM

GREAT PLAINS CONSERVATION PROGRAM

For necessary expenses to carry into effect a program of conservation in the Great Plains area, pursuant to section 16(b) of the Soil Conservation and Domestic Allotment Act, as added by the Act of August 7, 1956, as amended (16 U.S.C. 590p(b)), $25,271,000, to remain available until expended. (16 U.S.C. 590p(b)(7)). *(7 U.S.C. 2201-02; Agriculture, Rural Development, Food and Drug Administration, and Related Agencies Appropriations Act, 1992.)*

PROGRAM AND FINANCING (IN THOUSANDS OF DOLLARS)

Identification code 12-2268-0-1-302	1991 actual	1992 est.	1993 est.
Program by activities			
Direct program:			
00.01 Cost-sharing assistance	14,382	17,868	16,179
00.02 Cost-sharing programming and contract administration	2,778	2,909	2,909
00.03 Technical assistance	5,905	6,183	6,183
00.91 Total direct program	23,065	26,960	25,271
01.01 Reimbursable program	13	20	20
10.00 Total obligations	23,078	26,980	25,291
Financing:			
21.40 Unobligated balance available, start of year	-117	-1,689	....
24.40 Unobligated balance available, end of year	1,689	....	....
39.00 **Budget authority (gross)**	**24,650**	**25,291**	**25,291**
Budget authority:			
Current:			
40.00 **Appropriation**	**24,637**	**25,271**	**25,271**
Permanent:			
68.00 **Spending authority from offsetting collections (new)**	**13**	**20**	**20**
Relation of obligations to outlays:			
71.00 Total obligations	23,078	26,980	25,291
72.40 Obligated balance, start of year	36,495	37,511	41,843
74.40 Obligated balance, end of year	-37,511	-41,843	-41,808
87.00 Outlays (gross)	22,062	22,648	25,326
Adjustments to budget authority and outlays:			
Deductions for offsetting collections			
88.00 Federal funds	-13	-16	-16
88.40 Non-Federal sources	....	-4	-4
88.90 Total, offsetting collections	-13	-20	-20
89.00 Budget authority (net)	24,637	25,271	25,271
90.00 Outlays (net)	22,049	22,628	25,306

Source: Budget of the United States Government, Fiscal Year 1993, "Detailed Budget Estimates", p. A1-288.

EXAMPLE OF PROGRAM AND FINANCING SCHEDULE PRECEDED BY APPROPRIATIONS LANGUAGE (EXECUTIVE BUDGET) FOR DEPARTMENT DEFENSE PROGRAM

OPERATION AND MAINTENANCE, NAVY RESERVE

For expenses, not otherwise provided for, necessary for the operation and maintenance, including training, organization, and administration of the Navy Reserve; repair of facilities and equipment; hire of passenger motor vehicles; travel and transportation; care of the dead; recruiting; procurement of services, supplies and equipment; and communications; [$825,500,000] *$852,700,000. (10 U.S.C. 262, 276, 503, 1481-88, 2110, 2202, 2231, 2233a, 2631-34, 5013, 5062, 5251, 6022; Department of Defense Appropriations Act, 1992; addditional authorizing legislation to be proposed.)*

[For an additional amount for "Operation and maintenance, Navy Reserve", $28,300,000.] *(Dire Emergency Supplemental Appropriations Act, 1992.)*

PROGRAM AND FINANCING (IN THOUSANDS OF DOLLARS)

Identification code 17-1806-0-1-051	1991 actual	1992 est.	1993 est.
Program by activities			
Direct program:			
00.01 Mission forces..............................	924,406	777,233	774,582
00.02 Depot maintenance..........................	85,675	93,457	71,116
00.03 Other support................................	6,632	6,810	7,002
00.91 Total direct program..........................	1,016,713	877,500	852,700
01.01 Reimbursable program........................	26,455	19,562	20,262
10.00 Total obligations	1,043,168	897,062	872,962
Financing:			
22.00 Unobligated balance transferred, net...........	....	-3,700	....
25.00 Unobligated balance expiring	5,317	....	....
39.00 **Budget authority (gross)**.....................	**1,048,485**	**893,362**	**872,962**
Budget authority:			
Current:			
40.00 Appropriation.............................	998,000	825,500	852,700
42.00 Transferred from other accounts...............	24,030	48,300	
Appropriations (total)......................	1,022,030	873,800	852,700
Permanent:			
68.00 **Spending authority from offsetting collections (new)**................................	**26,455**	**19,562**	**20,262**
Relation of obligations to outlays:			
71.00 Total obligations..........................	1,043,168	897,062	872,962
72.40 Obligated balance, start of year...................	461,988	501,501	481,551
74.40 Obligated balance, end of year.....................	-501,501	-481,551	-495,376
77.00 Adjustments in expired accounts........	-26,656	....	....
87.00 Outlays (gross)	976,999	917,012	859,137
Adjustments to budget authority and outlays:			
Deductions for offsetting collections			
88.00 Federal funds............................	-24,619	-18,116	-18,764
88.30 Trust funds	-22	....	....
88.40 Non-Federal sources.............................	-1,814	-1,446	-1,498
88.90 Total, offsetting collections.................	-26,455	-19,562	-20,262
89.00 Budget authority (net)......................	1,022,030	873,800	852,700
90.00 Outlays (net).............................	950,544	897,450	838,875

Source: Budget of the United States Government, Fiscal Year 1993, "Detailed Budget Estimates", p. Two-32

TERMS AND DEFINITIONS

ACCOUNT

A separate financial reporting unit for budget, management, and/or accounting purposes. All budgetary transactions are recorded in accounts, but not all accounts are budgetary in nature (that is, some accounts do not directly affect the budget but are used purely for accounting purposes). Budget (and off-budget) accounts are used to record all transactions within the budget (or off-budget), whereas other accounts (such as deposit fund, credit financing, and foreign currency accounts) are used for accounting purposes connected with funds that are nonbudgetary in nature. The Budget Enforcement Act defines "account" as an item for which appropriations are made in any appropriation act; for items not provided for in appropriation acts, "account" means an item for which there is a designated budget account identification code number in the President's budget. *(See also* Credit Reform Act Accounts *under* Credit Reform.)

ACCOUNT IN THE PRESIDENT'S BUDGET: EXPENDITURE/APPROPRIATION AND RECEIPT ACCOUNTS CLASSIFIED BY FUND TYPES

Accounts used by the federal government to record outlays (expenditure accounts) and income (receipt accounts) primarily for budgeting or management information purposes but also for accounting purposes. All budget (and offbudget) accounts are classified as being either expenditure or receipt (including offsetting receipt) accounts and by fund group. Budget (and off-budget) transactions fall within either of two fund groups: (1) federal funds and (2) trust funds.

All federal fund and trust fund accounts are included within the budget (that is, they are on-budget) unless they are excluded from the budget by law. Federal and trust funds excluded from the budget by law are classified as being off-budget. The term *off-budget* differs from the term *non-budgetary*. Non-budgetary refers to activities (such as the credit financing accounts) that do not belong in the budget under existing concepts, while off-budget refers to accounts that belong on-budget under budget concepts but that are excluded from the budget under terms of law.

FEDERAL FUND ACCOUNTS

Accounts composed of moneys collected and spent by the federal government other than those designated as trust funds. Federal fund accounts include general, special, public enterprise, and intragovernmental fund accounts.

General Fund Accounts

Federal fund accounts composed of all federal money not allocated to any other fund account.

General Fund Receipt Account.

A receipt account credited with all collections that are not earmarked by law for a specific purpose. These collections are presented in the *Budget of the United States Government* as either governmental (budget) receipts or offsetting receipts. These include taxes, customs duties, and miscellaneous receipts.

General Fund Expenditure Account.

An appropriation account established to record amounts appropriated by law for the general support of federal government activities and the subsequent expenditure of these funds. It includes spending from both annual and permanent appropriations.

Special Fund Accounts.

Federal fund accounts earmarked by law for a specific purpose.

Special Fund Receipt Account.

A receipt account credited with collections that are earmarked by law but included in the federal funds group rather than classified as trust fund collections. These collections are presented in the *Budget of the United States Government* as either governmental (budget) receipts or offsetting receipts. *(See also* Earmarking.)

Special Fund Expenditure Account.
An appropriation account established to record appropriations, obligations, and outlays financed by the proceeds of special fund receipts. *(See also* Earmarking.)

Public Enterprise Revolving Fund Accounts.

Expenditure accounts authorized by law to be credited with offsetting collections, primarily from the public, that are generated by and earmarked to finance a continuing cycle of business-type operations. Such funds may be financed in part from appropriations.

Intragovernmental Fund Accounts.

Expenditure accounts authorized by law to facilitate financing transactions primarily within and between federal agencies on a revolving fund basis.

Intragovernmental Revolving Fund Account
An appropriation account authorized to be credited with collections, primarily from other agencies and accounts, that are earmarked to finance a continuing cycle of business-type operations, including working capital funds, industrial funds, stock funds, and supply funds. *(See also* Working Capital Fund.)

Management Fund Account.
An account authorized by law to credit collections from two or more appropriations to finance activity not involving a continuing cycle of business-type operations. Such accounts do not generally own a significant amount of assets such as supplies, equipment, or loans, nor do they have a specified amount of capital provided--a corpus. The Navy Management Fund is an example of such an account.
Consolidated Working Fund Accounts are a subset of management funds. These are special working funds established under the authority of Section 601 of the Economy Act (31 U.S.C. 1535, 1536) to receive advance payments from other agencies or accounts. Consolidated working fund accounts are not used to finance the work directly but only to reimburse the appropriation or fund account that will finance the work to be performed. Amounts in consolidated working fund accounts are available for the same periods as those of the accounts advancing the funds. Consolidated working fund accounts are

shown as separate accounts on the books of Treasury, but are not separately identified in the President's budget. Transactions of these accounts are included in the presentation of the appropriation or fund account actually performing the service or providing the materials.

TRUST FUND ACCOUNTS

Accounts designated as "trust funds" by law, regardless of any other meaning of the words "trust fund." A trust fund account is usually either a receipt or an expenditure account. A trust revolving fund, however, receives offsetting collections authorized to be credited to an expenditure account. *(See also* Earmarking.)

Trust Fund Receipt Account.
A receipt account credited with collections classified as trust fund collections. These collections are presented as either governmental (on-budget or off-budget) receipts or offsetting receipts.

Trust Fund Expenditure Account.
An appropriation account established to record amounts appropriated to finance programs specified by law as being trust funds. Such funds may be on-budget or off-budget.

Trust Revolving Fund Account.
A trust fund expenditure account that is an appropriation account authorized to be credited with collections and used to carry out a cycle of business-type operations in accordance with statute.

ACCOUNT IN TREASURY'S ANNUAL REPORT APPENDIX: APPROPRIATION AND FISCAL YEAR ACCOUNTS CLASSIFIED BY FUND TYPES

An account established in the Treasury that records appropriations and other budgetary resources provided to it by appropriations and authorizations statutes and transactions affecting the account.

In some respects, these accounts are different from the accounts in the President's budget. Unlike those in the President's budget, they do not include expenditure accounts. In addition, Treasury establishes a separate account for each annual, multiyear, or no-year appropriation and identifies it by a designation of the fiscal year(s) for which amounts are available for obligation. However, for the purposes of presentation of data in the President's budget, appropriations to an account with the same or similar titles for the years covered by the budget are considered to be a single account.

ACCOUNTS FOR PURPOSES OTHER THAN BUDGET PRESENTATION

DEPOSIT FUND ACCOUNTS

Nonbudgetary accounts established to account for collections that are either (a) held temporarily and later refunded or paid upon administrative or legal determination as to the proper disposition thereof or (b) held by the government as banker or agent for others and paid out at the direction of the depositor. Examples include savings accounts for military personnel; state and local income taxes withheld from federal employees' salaries; and payroll deductions for the purchase of savings bonds by civilian employees of the government. Deposit fund balances are accounted for as liabilities of the federal government. These accounts are not included in the budget totals because the amounts are not available for government purposes. However, since the cash in the accounts is used by Treasury to satisfy immediate cash requirements of the government, to the extent that they are not invested in federal debt, changes in deposit fund balances are shown as a means of financing the deficit in the budget.

FOREIGN CURRENCY FUND ACCOUNTS

Accounts established in Treasury for foreign currency that is acquired without payment of United States dollars. An example of such accounts are those set up through the Agricultural Trade Development and Assistance Act (7 U.S.C. 1691-1736g).

RECEIPT CLEARING ACCOUNTS

Accounts set up to hold general, special, or trust fund receipts temporarily, pending credit to the applicable federal or trust fund receipt accounts.

TRANSFER APPROPRIATION ACCOUNTS

Accounts established to receive and disburse allocations. Such allocations and transfers are not adjustments to budget authority or balances of budget authority. Rather, the transactions and any adjustments therein are treated as nonexpenditure transfers at the time the allocation is made. The accounts carry symbols that identify the original appropriation from which moneys have been advanced. Transfer appropriation accounts are symbolized by adding the receiving agency's department prefix to the original appropriation or fund account symbol. In some cases, a bureau suffix is added to show that the transfer is being made to a particular bureau within the receiving department. For budget purposes, transactions in the transfer accounts are reported with the transactions in the parent accounts. *(See also* Allocation; Nonexpenditure Transfer *under* Transfer.)

ACCOUNTS LISTED IN THE STANDARD GENERAL LEDGER

See under Standard General Ledger Chart of Accounts

ACCOUNTS PAYABLE

Amounts owed to others for goods and services received, assets acquired, and amounts received but not yet earned. For reporting purposes, according to OMB Circular A-34, "accounts payable, net," consists of (a) the amount owed by an account for goods received and services performed but not yet paid for, (b) the amount of income that has been received by an account but not yet earned, and (c) as offsets, accounts receivable and the amount of advances made by the account for which goods have not yet been received or services performed. *(See also* Accounts Receivable.)

ACCOUNTS RECEIVABLE

Amounts due from others for goods furnished and services rendered. Such amounts include reimbursements earned and refunds receivable. *(See also* Accounts Payable.)

ACCRUED EXPENDITURE

See under Expended Appropriations

ADJUSTMENTS TO DISCRETIONARY SPENDING LIMITS (BUDGET ENFORCEMENT ACT TERM)

Changes in discretionary spending limits calculated by the Office of Management and Budget for certain purposes specified in the Budget Enforcement Act. Such adjustments must be made and reported in the discretionary sequestration reports issued by CBO and OMB and in the President's budget. *(See* Appropriations *under* Budget Authority; Budget Enforcement Act; Preview Reports *under* Sequestration Reports; Emergency Legislation.)

ADJUSTMENT FOR CHANGES IN CONCEPTS AND DEFINITIONS

An adjustment to discretionary spending limits due to differences between baseline levels of outlays and new budget authority calculated using old concepts and definitions and those levels calculated using new concepts and definitions. Some changes in concepts and definitions, such as credit reform and the redefinition of budget authority to include authority to collect offsetting receipts, arose from the Budget Enforcement Act. Proposed changes that are not a result of the Budget Enforcement Act must be made in consultation with the House and Senate Committees on Appropriations and the Budget, the House Committee on Government Operations and the Senate Committee on Governmental Affairs. *(See also* Budget Authority; Credit Reform.)

ADJUSTMENT FOR CHANGES IN INFLATION

An adjustment to discretionary spending limits due to differences between actual inflation and the amount originally assumed in the Budget Enforcement Act (BEA). The adjustment compensates for inflation and misestimates of inflation at the time BEA was enacted. The act states that inflation is to be measured by the average estimated gross national product implicit price deflator index for the fiscal year divided by the average index for the prior fiscal year. *(See also* Budget Enforcement Act; Implicit Price Deflator; and Inflator.)

ADJUSTMENT FOR SPECIAL ALLOWANCE FOR DISCRETIONARY NEW BUDGET AUTHORITY

Under the Budget Enforcement Act, an adjustment required to be made by OMB to the discretionary spending limits for new budget authority and associated outlays by specified amounts in the domestic and international categories. The Budget Enforcement Act sets forth formulas for calculating the special allowances. (*See also* Category of Discretionary Spending.)

ADJUSTMENT FOR SPECIAL OUTLAY ALLOWANCE

An increase in the outlay limit required by the Budget Enforcement Act if outlays exceed a discretionary spending limit but new budget authority does not exceed that limit. The act specifies separate special outlay allowances by category for fiscal years 1991,1992, and 1993. For fiscal years 1994 and 1995, the act provides an allowance for total discretionary spending. This special allowance is intended to insulate the legislative process from estimating differences between CBO and OMB. (*See also* Category of Discretionary Spending.)

AS-USED ADJUSTMENT

An adjustment to discretionary spending limits that arises only to the extent that an amount is appropriated for a certain purpose. Such an adjustment includes those made for the following purposes: additional funding for the Internal Revenue Service (within stated ceilings), debt of Egypt and Poland forgiven in calendar years 1990 and 1991, credit reestimates, additional funding for the International Monetary Fund and for emergency appropriations.

ADJUSTMENTS TO MAXIMUM DEFICIT AMOUNTS (BUDGET ENFORCEMENT ACT TERM)

Changes by the President to the deficit target (known as the "maximum deficit amount" and set forth by the Congressional Budget Act, as amended) to reflect up-to-date reestimates of economic and technical assumptions and any changes in concepts and definitions. In the budget for fiscal years 1992 and 1993, the President must adjust the maximum deficit amount for the budget year and the outyears through

1995. The President may choose to adjust the maximum deficit amount for technical and economic assumptions and changes in concepts and definitions in fiscal year 1994. An adjustment for fiscal year 1995 may not be made unless there has already been an adjustment for fiscal year 1994. The maximum deficit amount must be adjusted by the amount of the adjustment to the discretionary spending limits applicable for each fiscal year. *(See also* Adjustments to Discretionary Spending Limits; Maximum Deficit Amount; Outyear; Up-to-Date.)

ADMINISTRATIVE DIVISION OR SUBDIVISION OF FUNDS

Any distribution of an appropriation or fund made pursuant to the Antideficiency Act (31 U.S.C. 1512 and 1514). Overobligation or overexpenditure of the following administrative divisions of funds are always violations of the Antideficiency Act: apportionments, allotments, and suballotments. *(See also* Allotment; Antideficiency Act; Antideficiency Act Violation; Apportionment; Limitation.)

ADVANCE

An amount paid prior to the later receipt of goods, services, or other assets. Advances are ordinarily made only to payees to whom an agency has an obligation, and they do not exceed the amount of the obligation. A common example is a travel advance, which is an amount made available to an employee prior to the beginning of a trip for costs incurred in accordance with the Travel Expense Act of 1949 (5 U.S.C. 5705) and in accordance with standardized government travel regulations. *(See also* Undelivered Orders.)

ADVANCE APPROPRIATION

Budget authority provided in an appropriation act which is first available in a fiscal year beyond the fiscal year for which the appropriation act is enacted. The amount is not included in the budget totals of the year for which the appropriation bill is enacted but rather in those for the fiscal year in which the amount will become available for obligation. (For a distinction, *see* Advance Funding; Multiple-Year Authority *under* Duration *under* Budget Authority.)

ADVANCE FUNDING

Budget authority provided in an appropriation act to obligate and disburse (outlay) in the current fiscal year funds from a succeeding year's appropriation. The funds so obligated increase the budget authority for the fiscal year during which they are obligated and decrease it for the succeeding fiscal year. Advance funding is a means to avoid making supplemental requests late in the fiscal year for certain entitlement programs in cases where the appropriations for the current year prove to be insufficient. (For a distinction, *see* Advance Appropriation; Multiple-Year Authority *under* Duration *under* Budget Authority.)

AGENCY

Under the broadest definition of the term, a department, agency, or instrumentality of the U.S. government (31 U.S.C. 101). However, statutes or regulations often include specific definitions of the term "agency" (or related terms like "executive agency" or "federal agency") which delineate their effect. For example, the provisions of the Budget and Accounting Act of 1921, which relate to the preparation of the President's budget, specifically define "agency" to include the District of Columbia government but exclude the legislative branch or the Supreme Court (31 U.S.C. 1101), even though the budget of the District of Columbia government is excluded from the federal budget, whereas the legislative and judicial branches are treated as agencies for purposes of the budget.

AGENCY MISSION

Responsibility assigned to a specific agency for meeting national needs. An agency mission expresses the purpose of the programs of that agency and its component organizations. National needs are generally described in the context of the budget functional classification system as major functions, while agency missions are generally described in the context of subfunctions. (*See also* Functional Classification; Mission Budgeting; National Needs.)

ALLOCATION

For the purposes of budgeting, an allocation is the amount of budget authority transferred from one agency, bureau, or account that is set aside in a transfer appropriation account to carry out the purposes of the parent appropriation or fund. (The appropriation or fund from which the allocation is made is called the parent appropriation or fund.) For example, an allocation is made when one or more agencies share the administration of a program for which appropriations are made to only one of the agencies or to the President. Transactions involving allocation accounts appear in the Object Classification Schedule, with the corresponding Program and Financing Schedule, in the *Budget of the United States Government*. (For detailed discussion on the treatment of Object Classification—With Allocation Accounts, *see* OMB Circular A-1 1, revised. *See also* Object Classification; Transfer; Transfer Appropriation Accounts *under* Account for Purposes Other Than Budget Presentation.)

For purposes of section 302(a) and 602(a) of the Congressional Budget and Impoundment Control Act of 1974 (2 U.S.C. 633), an allocation is the distribution of spending authority and outlays to relevant committees based on the levels contained in a concurrent resolution on the budget. *(See also* Committee Allocation.)

ALLOTMENT

An authorization by either the agency head or another authorized employee to his/ her subordinates to incur obligations within a specified amount. Each agency makes allotments pursuant to specific procedures it establishes within the general requirements stated in OMB Circular A-34. The amount allotted by an agency cannot exceed the amount apportioned by the Office of Management and Budget. *(See also* Administrative Division or Subdivision of Funds; Apportionment; Reapportionment.)

ALLOWANCE

An amount included in the President's budget request or included in a projection in a congressional resolution on the budget to cover possible additional proposals, such as contingencies for programs whose expenditures are controllable only by statutory change and other requirements. As used by the Congress in the concurrent resolutions on the budget, an allowance represents a special functional classification designed to include an amount to cover possible requirements. An allowance remains undistributed until the contingency on which it is based occurs; then it is distributed to the appropriate functional classification. For agency budgetary accounting and fund control purposes, an allowance is a subdivision of an allotment. (For treatment of undistributed allowances, *see* function 920 in "Federal Programs by Function" in the *Budget of the United States Government.)* (For more details on the government accounting definition, *see U.S Government Standard General Ledger.) (See also* Adjustments for Special Allowance for Discretionary New Budget Authority and Adjustment for Special Outlay Allowance *under* Adjustments to Discretionary Spending Limits.)

ANTIDEFICIENCY ACT

Enacted legislation which

- prohibits the making of expenditures or the incurring of obligations prior to appropriations,
- prohibits the incurring of obligations or the making of expenditures (outlays) in excess of amounts available in appropriation or fund accounts unless specifically authorized by law (31 U.S.C. 1341(a)),
- requires agencies to apportion appropriated funds and other budgetary resources (31 U.S.C. 1512),
- requires a system of administrative controls within each agency (see 31 U.S.C. 1514 for the administrative divisions established),
- prohibits incurring any obligation or making any expenditure (outlay) in excess of an apportionment or reapportionment or in excess of other subdivisions established pursuant to 31 U.S.C. 1513 and 1514 (31 U.S.C. 1517),
- specifies penalties for antideficiency violations *(see* Antideficiency Act Violation),
- requires the apportionment of appropriation or fund accounts to prevent the need for a supplemental or deficiency appropriation, and
- assists in bringing about the most effective and economical use of appropriations and funds (31 U.S.C. 1512-1519).

The act permits agencies to reserve funds (that is, withhold them from obligation) under certain circumstances. *(See also* Administrative Division or Subdivision of Funds; Antideficiency Act

Violation; Apportionment; Budgetary Reserves; Deficiency Apportionment; Deficiency Appropriation; Expenditure; Fund Accounting.)

ANTIDEFICIENCY ACT VIOLATION

An Antideficiency Act violation occurs when one or more of the following occurs:

- overobligation or overexpenditure of an appropriation or fund account (31 U.S.C. 1341(a));
- entering into a contract or making an obligation in advance of an appropriation, unless specifically authorized by law (31 U.S.C. 1341(a));
- acceptance of voluntary service, unless authorized by law (31 U.S.C. 1342); or
- overobligation or overexpenditure of (1) an apportionment or reapportionment or (2) amounts permitted by the administrative control of funds regulations (31 U.S.C. 1517(a)).

Penalties for Antideficiency Act violations include administrative discipline, such as suspension from duty without pay or removal from office. In addition, an officer or employee convicted of willfully and knowingly violating the law shall be fined not more than $5,000, imprisoned for not more than 2 years, or both (31 U.S.C. 1349,1350,1518, and 1519). (*See also* Administrative Division or Subdivision of Funds; Antideficiency Act; Expenditure.)

APPENDIX TO TREASURY'S ANNUAL REPORT

An annual statement of budgetary results on a cash basis presented at the individual receipt and appropriation account level. The appendix is published as a separate document. It supports in detail the fiscal year-end results published in the *Monthly Treasury Statement*. (*See also* Monthly Treasury Statement.)

APPORTIONMENT

The action by which OMB distributes amounts available for obligation, including budgetary reserves established pursuant to law, in an appropriation or fund account. An apportionment divides amounts available for obligation by specific time periods (usually quarters), activities, projects, objects, or a combination thereof. The amounts so apportioned limit the amount of obligations that may be incurred. In apportioning any account, some funds may be reserved to provide for contingencies or to effect savings, pursuant to the Antideficiency Act Funds, including Antideficiency Act reserves, may also be proposed for deferral or rescission pursuant to the Impoundment Control Act of 1974 (2 U.S.C. 681-688).

The apportionment process is intended to (1) prevent the obligation of amounts available within an appropriation or fund account in a manner that would require deficiency or supplemental appropriations and (2) achieve the most effective and economical use of amounts made available for obligation. *(See also* Administrative Division or Subdivision of Funds; Allotment; Antideficiency Act; Appropriated Entitlement; Budgetary Reserves; Deferral of Budget Authority; Deficiency Apportionment; Deficiency Appropriation; Limitation; Reapportionment; Rescission; Supplemental Appropriation.)

APPROPRIATED ENTITLEMENT

An entitlement whose budget authority is provided in an annual appropriation act. Such entitlements require annual appropriations but are beyond the effective control of the appropriations process because of statutory eligibility and benefit criteria. The food stamp program is an example of such an entitlement. *(See also* Apportionment; Entitlement Authority.)

APPROPRIATION ACT

A statute, under the jurisdiction of the House and Senate Committees on Appropriations, that generally provides legal authority for federal agencies to incur obligations and to make payments out of Treasury for specified purposes. An appropriation act fulfills the requirement of Article I, section 9 of the Constitution, which provides that "no money shall be drawn from the Treasury, but in Consequence of Appropriations made by Law." Consequently, even entitlements must be funded by appropriations; however, such appropriations (often permanent, indefinite ones that are not under the jurisdiction of the appropriations committees) may be created by authorizing legislation. An appropriation act generally follows enactment of authorizing legislation unless the authorizing legislation provides budget authority. *(See also* Appropriations *under* Forms of Budget Authority *under* Budget Authority; Authorizing Legislation; Limitation.)

The three major types of appropriation acts are regular, supplemental, and continuing. Regular appropriation acts are all appropriation acts that are not supplemental or continuing. Currently, 13 regular appropriation acts are considered annually. From time to time, supplemental appropriation acts are also enacted. When action on regular appropriation bills is not completed before the beginning of the fiscal year, a continuing resolution or bill may be enacted to provide funding for the affected agencies for the full year, up to a specified date, or until their regular appropriations are enacted. *(See also* Continuing Appropriations *under* Extensions of Budget Authority *under* Budget Authority; Supplemental Appropriations.)

ASSET

A probable future economic benefit obtained or controlled by the government as a result of past transactions or events. Assets may be tangible or intangible and are expressed in terms of cost or some other value. *(See also* Liability.)

ASSET SALE/LOAN PREPAYMENT

The sale of a physical or financial asset by the federal government. Revenue from the sale of assets is accounted for in the budget as offsetting receipts or collections. A loan prepayment occurs when the borrower repays, with or without a penalty, the principal and interest of a loan held by the government prior to the contractually scheduled date of repayment.

In general, asset sales and loan prepayments increase current cash payments received by the government at the expense of a stream of future income that the government would otherwise receive. Gramm-Rudman-Hollings (2 U.S.C. 907(e)) provides that the proceeds of most of those asset sales or loan prepayments which are (1) not mandated by law prior to September 18, 1987, or (2) not consistent with operations in fiscal year 1986 shall not count as deficit reduction for purposes of estimating the Gramm-Rudman-Hollings baseline deficit, although such proceeds do count for other budgetary purposes. *(See also* Direct Loan.)

AUTHORIZING COMMITTEE

A standing committee of the House or Senate with legislative jurisdiction over the subject matter of those laws, or parts of laws, that set up or continue the operations of federal programs or agencies. An authorizing committee also has jurisdiction in those instances where backdoor authority is provided in the substantive legislation. *(See also* Backdoor Authority/Backdoor Spending; Oversight Committee; Spending Committee.)

AUTHORIZING LEGISLATION

Substantive legislation that sets up or continues the operation of a federal program or agency either indefinitely or for a specific period of time or that sanctions a particular type of obligation or expenditure within a program.

Authorizing legislation is normally a prerequisite for appropriations. It may place a limit on the amount of budget authority to be included in appropriation acts or it may authorize the appropriation of "such sums as may be necessary." In some instances, authorizing legislation may provide authority to incur debts or may mandate payment to particular persons or political subdivisions of the country. *(See also* Appropriation Act; Backdoor Authority/Backdoor Spending; Entitlement Authority; Limitation; Substantive Law.)

AUTOMATIC SPENDING INCREASE (BUDGET ENFORCEMENT ACT TERM)

For the purposes of calculating a sequestration under the Budget Enforcement Act of 1990, an increase in outlays in a specifically designated program due to a change in an index, not a change in law. (2 U.S.C. 906 (a)). Such an increase may be reduced by sequestration. In those programs all amounts other than the automatic spending increase are exempt from reduction under a sequestration order. Under current law three programs-the National Wool Act, the special milk program, and the vocational rehabilitation basic state grants-are included under this provision. Many federal programs automatically increase their budgetary resources by law, but these increases are not defined as "automatic spending increases" and, therefore, sequestration may not reduce them or may not reduce them by the full uniform reduction percentage. *(See also* Gramm-Rudman-Hollings; Sequestration; Special Rules; Uniform Reduction Percentage.)

BACKDOOR AUTHORITY/BACKDOOR SPENDING

A collective designation for authority provided in laws other than appropriation acts to obligate the government to make payments. It includes contract authority, authority to borrow, and entitlement authority for which the budget authority is not provided in advance by appropriation acts. It also includes authority to forgo the collection of proprietary offsetting receipts and to make any other payments for which the budget authority is not provided in advance by appropriation acts. (For the statutorily defined equivalent term, *see* Spending Authority. *See also* Appropriations and Contract Authority *under* Budget Authority; Authorizing Legislation; Entitlement Authority; Spending Committee.)

BALANCED BUDGET

A budget in which receipts equal outlays. (*See also* Deficit; Surplus.)

BASELINE

An estimate of spending, revenue, the deficit or surplus, and the public debt expected during a fiscal year under current laws and current policy. For the purposes of the Budget Enforcement Act, the baseline is defined as the projection of current-year levels of new budget authority; outlays, revenues, and the surplus or deficit into the budget year and outyears based on laws enacted through the applicable date. Section 257 of Gramm-Rudman-Hollings sets forth rules for calculating the baseline.. (*See also* Projections.)

CBO BASELINE

The Congressional Budget Office's baseline for the upcoming fiscal year. This baseline shows the pattern of federal government revenues and expenditures for the next 5 years if current policies continue. It appears in CBO's annual report for the Budget Committees on the economic and budget outlook for the upcoming year. The CBO baseline is revised, as necessary, once the President's budget is released. It is also modified, as necessary, to conform to new legislative requirements, such as those imposed by the Gramm-Rudman-Hollings Act and the Budget Enforcement Act.

BASES OF BUDGETING

Methods for calculating budget figures. Not all methods are mutually exclusive. For example, the federal budget includes both net and gross figures and reports both obligations and cash or cash equivalent spending. As a general rule, budget receipts and outlays are on a cash or cash equivalent basis however, interest on public issues of public debt is recorded on an accrual basis. (*See also* Capital Budget.)

CASH OR CASH EQUIVALENT BASIS

The basis whereby receipts are recorded when received and expenditures are recorded when paid, without regard to the accounting period in which the receipts are earned or the costs incurred. "Cash" generally refers to payment by cash, checks, or electronic funds transfers. "Cash equivalent" refers to the use of an instrument or process that creates a substitute for cash. For example, when the government issues a debt instrument of any kind in satisfaction of claims, the transaction is recorded as simultaneous outlays and borrowing—the outlays when the debt instrument is issued, not when it is redeemed. Capital leases (that is, capital acquisitions through lease-purchases) are treated as cash equivalent outlays and borrowing (or borrowing equivalents).

OBLIGATIONS BASIS

The basis whereby financial transactions involving the use of funds are recorded in the accounts primarily when goods and services are ordered, regardless of when the resources acquired are to be received or consumed.

ACCRUAL BASIS

The basis whereby transactions and events are recognized when they occur, regardless of when cash is received or paid.

BUDGETING IN RELATION TO TOTALS

Gross Basis.

In customary usage, "gross" refers to the sum or total value of a transaction before reduction of applicable offsets. The gross basis of budgeting refers to budgetary totals from which offsetting collections have not been deducted. Under this display, totals include obligations and expenditures from offsetting collections along with governmental receipts rather than as offsets to outlays. *(See also* Offsetting Collections and Offsetting Receipts *under* Collections.)

Net Basis.

The use of budgetary totals from which offsetting collections have been deducted. Under this display, budgetary totals include offsetting collections as offsets to obligations and outlays rather than as receipts. *(See also* Offsetting Collections *under* Collections.)

BIENNIAL BUDGET

A budget covering a period of 2 years. The federal government has an annual budget, but biennial budget proposals have been made. The 2-year period can apply to the budget presented to the Congress by the President, to the budget resolution adopted by the Congress, or to appropriations measures. The 1985 Defense Authorization Act mandated biennial budgeting for the Department of Defense on an experimental basis beginning with the budgets for 1988 and 1989; however, to date appropriations have been made on an annual basis.

BREACH (BUDGET ENFORCEMENT ACT TERM)

For any fiscal year, the amount by which new budget authority or outlays for that year (within a category of discretionary appropriations) is above that category's discretionary spending limit for new budget authority or outlays for that year. The act provides for sequestration of budgetary resources to eliminate breaches. *(See also* Discretionary Spending Sequestration under Sequestration; Discretionary Sequestration Report *under* Sequestration Reports.)

BUDGET ACTIVITY

A specific and distinguishable line of work performed by a governmental unit to discharge a function or subfunction for which the governmental unit is responsible. Activities within most accounts identify the purposes, projects, or types of activities financed. For example, food inspection is an activity performed in the discharge of the health function. A budget activity is presented in the Program by Activities section in the Program and Financing Schedule for each account in the *Budget of the United States Government. (See also* Functional Classification; for a partial distinction, *see* Program, Project, or Activity.)

BUDGET AMENDMENT

A revision to a pending budget request which the President submits to the Congress before the Congress completes appropriations action.

BUDGET AUTHORITY

Authority provided by law to enter into financial obligations that will result in immediate or future outlays involving federal government funds. Budget authority includes the credit subsidy cost for direct loan and loan guarantee programs, but does not include authority to insure or guarantee the repayment of indebtedness incurred by another person or government. The basic forms of budget authority include (1) appropriations, (2) borrowing authority, (3) contract authority, and (4) authority to obligate and expend offsetting receipts and collections. Budget authority may be classified by its duration (1-year, multiple-year, or no-year), by the timing of the legislation providing the authority (current or permanent), by the manner of determining the amount available (definite or indefinite), or by its availability for new obligations. *(See also* Current Level Estimate.)

FORMS OF BUDGET AUTHORITY

Appropriations.

Authority given to federal agencies to incur obligations and to make payments from Treasury for specified purposes. An appropriation act, the most common means of providing budget authority, usually follows the enactment of authorizing legislation, but in some cases the authorizing legislation itself provides the budget authority. *(See also* Backdoor Authority/Backdoor Spending.)

Appropriations do not represent cash actually set aside in Treasury for purposes specified in the appropriation act; they represent amounts that agencies may obligate during the period of time specified in the respective appropriation acts. Certain types of appropriations are not counted as budget authority because they do not provide authority to incur obligations. Among these are appropriations:

- to liquidate contract authority (legislation to provide funds to pay obligations incurred against contract authority),
- to redeem outstanding debt (legislation to provide funds for debt retirement), and
- to refund receipts.

(See also Appropriation Act; Discretionary; Expired Budget Authority *under* Availability for New Obligations; Mandatory.)

Borrowing Authority.

Authority that permits agencies to incur obligations and make payments to liquidate the obligations out of borrowed moneys. Usually the funds are borrowed from Treasury, but in a few cases agencies borrow directly from the public. Borrowing authority does not include Treasury's authority to borrow from the public or other sources. *(See also* Debt, Federal.)

Contract Authority.

Authority that permits obligations to be incurred in advance of appropriations or receipts. Contract authority is therefore unfunded and a subsequent appropriation or offsetting collection is needed to liquidate the obligations. *(See also* Backdoor Authority/Backdoor Spending.)

Offsetting Receipts and Collections.

Authority to obligate and expend the proceeds of offsetting receipts and collections. The Congressional Budget Act of 1974, as amended by the Budget Enforcement Act of 1990, defines offsetting receipts and collections as negative budget authority and the reductions thereof as positive budget authority.

DETERMINATION OF AMOUNT

Definite Authority.

Budget authority which is stated as a specific sum at the time the authority is granted. This type of authority, whether in an appropriation act or other law, includes authority stated as "not to exceed" a specified figure.

Indefinite Authority.

Budget authority of an unspecified amount of money. Indefinite budget authority (usually an appropriation) may be appropriated as all or part of the amount of proceeds from the sale of financial assets, the amount necessary to cover obligations associated with payments, the receipts from specified sources - the exact amount of which is determinable only at some future date—or it may be appropriated as "such sums as may be necessary" for a given purpose.

DURATION

One-Year (Annual) Authority.

Budget authority which is available for obligation only during a specific fiscal year and which expires, if not obligated, at the end of that time. It is also known as a "fiscal year" or "annual" budget authority. *(See also* Discretionary.)

Multiple-Year Authority.

Budget authority which is available for a specified period of time in excess of 1 fiscal year. This authority generally takes the form of 2-year, 3-year, etc., availability but may cover periods that do not coincide with the start or end of a fiscal year. For example, the authority may be available from July 1 of one year through September 30 of the following fiscal year, a period of 15 months. This type of multiple-year authority is sometimes referred to as "forward funding." (For a distinction, *see* Advance Appropriation; Advance Funding. *See also* Full Funding; Mandatory.)

No-Year Authority.

Budget authority that remains available for obligation for an indefinite period of time, usually until the objectives for which the authority was made available are attained. *(See also* Mandatory.)

EXTENSIONS OF BUDGET AUTHORITY

Reappropriation.

Statutory action to continue the availability, whether for the same or different purposes, of all or part of the unobligated portion of budget authority that has expired or would otherwise expire. Reappropriations are counted as budget authority in the first year for which the availability is extended. (For a distinction, *see* Restoration.)

Continuing Appropriation/Continuing Resolution.

Legislation that may be enacted to provide budget authority for federal agencies and/or specific activities to continue in operation when the Congress and the President have not completed action on appropriations by the beginning of the fiscal year. Until regular appropriations are enacted, continuing appropriations may take their place. Continuing appropriations usually are passed in the legislative form of joint resolutions. A continuing resolution may be enacted for the full year, up to a specified date, or until regular appropriations are enacted. A continuing resolution usually specifies a maximum rate at which the obligations may be incurred based on levels specified in the resolution. The resolution may state that obligations may not exceed the current rate or must be the lower of the amounts provided in the appropriations bills passed in the House or Senate. If enacted to cover the entire fiscal year, the resolution will usually specify amounts provided for each appropriation account. *(See also* Appropriation Act; Joint Resolution; Supplemental Appropriation.)

TIMING OF LEGISLATIVE ACTION

Current Authority.

Budget authority made available by the Congress in, or immediately prior to, the fiscal year or years during which the funds are available for obligation.

Permanent Authority.

Budget authority that is available as the result of previously enacted legislation and which does not require new legislation for the current year. Such budget authority can be the result of substantive legislation or appropriation acts. When budget authority is enacted that will be treated as permanent authority in subsequent years, it is treated as permanent authority the first year it becomes available, as well as in succeeding years.

AVAILABILITY FOR NEW OBLIGATIONS

Expired Budget Authority.

Budget authority which is no longer available to incur new obligations. Such authority is still available for 5 years after the account expires for the payment of those valid obligations which were incurred before the authority expired. Unobligated balances of expired budget authority remain available for 5 years after the account expires to cover adjustments to prior obligations or obligations that should have been but may not have been recorded at that time. (For a statutory reference, *see 31 U.S.C.* 1552 (a)(2). *See also* Expired Account; Unobligated Balance *under* Obligational Authority; Warrant.)

Unexpired Budget Authority.

Budget authority which is available for incurring new obligations.

BUDGET ENFORCEMENT ACT

Title XIII of the Omnibus Budget Reconciliation Act of 1990. These statutory provisions amended the Balanced Budget and Emergency Deficit Control Act of 1985 and related amendments (Gramm-Rudman-Hollings) and the Congressional Budget and Impoundment Control Act of 1974. The Budget Enforcement Act modified procedures and definitions for sequestration and deficit reduction, reformed budgetary credit accounting, maintained the off-budget status of the budgetary credit accounting, maintained the off-budget status of the Old Age Survivor's and Disability Insurance Trust Funds, and removed Social Security trust fund receipts and outlays from deficit and sequestration calculations. *(See also* Adjustments to Discretionary Spending Limits; Category of Discretionary Spending; Credit Reform; Direct Spending Authority; Gramm-Rudman-Hollings; Mandatory; Off-budget.)

BUDGET ESTIMATES

Estimates of budget authority, outlays, receipts, or other budget measures that cover the current, budget, and future years, as reflected in the President's budget and budget updates. *(See also* Budget Update.)

BUDGET PREPARATION SYSTEM (BPS)

A computer system used by OMB to collect and process much of the information required for preparing the budget.

BUDGET RECEIPTS

See under Governmental Receipts *under* Collections

BUDGET UPDATE

A revised estimate of budget authority, receipts, and outlays issued subsequent to the issuance of the President's budget. The President is required by provisions of the Congressional Budget and Impoundment Control Act of 1974 *(see* provisions of 31 U.S.C. 1105(d), 1106) to transmit such statements to the Congress by July 15 of each year; however, the President may also submit budget updates at other times during the fiscal year. *(See also* Budget Estimates.)

BUDGET YEAR

See under Fiscal Year

BUDGETARY RESERVES

Portions of budgetary resources set aside (withheld through apportionment) by OMB by authority of the Antideficiency Act (31

U.S.C. 1512) solely to provide for contingencies or effect savings. Such savings are made possible through changes in requirements or through greater efficiency of operations. Budgetary resources may also be set aside if specifically provided for by particular appropriation acts or other laws.

Except as specifically provided by law, no reserves shall be established other than as authorized under the Antideficiency Act (31 U.S.C. 1512). Reserves established are reported to the Congress in accordance with provisions in the Impoundment Control Act of 1974 (2 U.S.C. 681-688). *(See also* Antideficiency Act; Apportionment; Deferral of Budget Authority; Rescission.)

BUDGETARY RESOURCES

The forms of authority given to an agency allowing it to incur obligations. Budgetary resources include the following: new budget authority, unobligated balances, direct spending authority, and obligation limitations. *(See also* Budget Authority; Exempt Programs and Activities; Limitation; Sequestrable Resource.)

CAPITAL BUDGET

A budget that segregates capital investments from the operating budget's expenditures. In such a budget, the capital investments that are excluded from the operating budget do not count towards calculating the operating budget's surplus or deficit at the time the investment is made. States that use capital budgets normally finance the capital investment from borrowing and then charge amortization (interest and debt repayment) to the operating budget.

CATEGORY OF DISCRETIONARY SPENDING (BUDGET ENFORCEMENT ACT TERM)

Subsets of discretionary appropriations established by the Budget Enforcement Act for the purposes of discretionary spending sequestration and points of order in the Senate. These are defense, international, and domestic in fiscal years 1991, 1992, and 1993. For fiscal years 1994 and 1995, the act establishes a single category for total discretionary spending. The joint statement of managers accompanying the conference report on the Omnibus Budget Reconciliation Act of 1990 designates which discretionary accounts fall into each category. *(See also* Adjustment for Special Allowance for Discretionary New Budget Authority; Adjustment for Special Outlay Allowance; Budget Enforcement Act.)

CLOSED ACCOUNT

An appropriation account whose balance has been canceled. Once balances are canceled, the amounts are not available for obligation or expenditure for any purpose. An account available for a definite period (fixed appropriation account) is canceled 5 fiscal years after the period of availability for obligation ends. An account available for an indefinite period (no-year account) is canceled if (l) the head of the agency concerned or the President determines that the purposes for which the appropriation was made have been carried out and (2) no disbursement has been made against the appropriation for 2 consecutive fiscal years. *(See also* Expired Account; Obligational Authority.)

COHORT

A group of post-1991 direct loans or loan guarantees obligated or committed, respectively, in the same fiscal year, even if disbursements occur in a subsequent fiscal year. Pre-1992 direct loans that are modified will constitute a single cohort. Likewise, pre-1992 loan guarantees that are modified will constitute a cohort. *(See also* Credit Reform; Direct Loan; Financing Tranche; Guaranteed Loan.)

COLLECTIONS

Amounts received by the federal government during the fiscal year. Collections are classified into two major categories: (l) governmental receipts (also called budget receipts) and (2) offsetting collections. *(See also* Account in the President's Budget; Off-Budget; On-Budget; Revenue.)

GOVERNMENTAL RECEIPTS

Collections from the public based on the government's exercise of its sovereign powers, including collections from payments by participants in compulsory social insurance programs. Governmental receipts consist of receipts from taxes, duties, social insurance premiums, court fines, compulsory licenses, and deposits of earnings by the Federal

Reserve System. Gifts and contributions (as distinguished from payments for services or cost sharing deposits by state and local governments) are also counted as governmental receipts. Governmental receipts do not include offsetting receipts, which are treated as offsets to outlays. Total governmental receipts include those specifically designated as off-budget by provisions of law. Total governmental receipts are compared with total outlays in calculating the budget surplus or deficit. *(See also* Expenditure and Receipt Accounts under Account in the President's Budget; Gross Basis and Net Basis *under* Budgeting in Relation to Totals *under* Bases of Budgeting.)

OFFSETTING COLLECTIONS

All collections by government accounts from other government accounts and any collections from the public that are of a business-type or market-oriented nature. They are classified into two major categories: (1) collections credited to appropriation or fund accounts, and (2) offsetting receipts, which are amounts deposited in receipt accounts. For collections credited to appropriation or fund accounts (that is, all revolving funds and some appropriation accounts), laws authorize collections to be credited directly to expenditure accounts and may make them available for obligation to meet the account's purpose without further legislative action. However, it is not uncommon for annual appropriations acts to include limitations on the obligations to be financed by these collections.

Offsetting receipts cannot be used without being appropriated. However, a significant portion of such collections, for example, most trust fund offsetting receipts, are permanently appropriated and, therefore, can be used without subsequent appropriation legislation. The Congressional Budget Act of 1974, as amended by the Budget Enforcement Act of 1990, defines offsetting receipts and collections as negative budget authority and the reductions thereof as positive budget authority. *(See also* Earmarking; Reimbursements.)

COLLECTIONS CREDITED TO APPROPRIATION OR FUND ACCOUNTS.

These include two categories:

Reimbursements.

When authorized by law, amounts collected for materials or services furnished to the public or other government accounts are treated as reimbursements to appropriations. (For accounting purposes, earned reimbursements are also known as revenues.) These offsetting collections are netted against gross outlays in determining net outlays from such appropriations. *(See also* Unfilled Customer Orders.)

Revolving Fund Collections.

In all three types of revolving funds—public enterprise, intragovernmental, and trust revolving—offsetting collections are netted against spending, and outlays are reported as the net amount.

OFFSETTING RECEIPTS.

Offsetting collections which are deposited in general, special, or trust fund receipt accounts. These receipts generally are deducted from budget authority and outlays by subfunction and by agency, but some are undistributed and are deducted from total budget authority and outlays. Offsetting receipts are subdivided into three categories: (1) intragovernmental transactions, (2) offsetting governmental receipts, and (3) proprietary receipts from the public.

Intragovernmental Transactions.

Payments into receipt accounts from governmental appropriations or fund accounts. They are treated as offsets to budget authority and outlays rather than as governmental receipts.

Intragovernmental transactions may be (1) intrabudgetary (on-budget), (2) offbudget, or (3) transactions between on-budget and off-budget accounts. Normally, intragovernmental transactions are deducted from both outlays and budget authority for the subfunction and agency receiving the payment. However, an agency's payment as an employer into employee retirement trust funds and interest received by trust funds appear as offsets to total budget authority and outlays for the government, rather than offsets at the agency level.

Intrabudgetary transactions are further subdivided into three categories: (1) interfund transactions, where the payment is from one fund group, either federal or trust, to a receipt account in the other fund group, (2) federal intrafund transactions, where the payment and receipt both occur within the federal fund group, and (3) trust intrafund transactions, where the payment and receipt both occur within the trust fund group.

Offsetting Governmental Receipts.

These receipts are governmental in nature but are required by law to be treated as offsetting. Currently, receipts in this category include foreign cash contributions for the costs of Operation Desert Shield/Desert Storm.

Proprietary Receipts From the Public.

Collections from outside the government which are deposited in receipt accounts that arise as a result of the government's business-type or market-oriented activities. Among these are interest received, proceeds from the sale of property and products, charges for nonregulatory services, and rents and royalties. Such collections may be credited to general fund, special fund, or trust fund receipt accounts and are offset against budget authority and outlays. In most cases, such offsets are by agency and by subfunction but some proprietary receipts are deducted from total budget authority and outlays for the government as a whole. An example of the latter is rents and royalties on the Outer Continental Shelf. *(See* Subfunction 953 in appendix II. *See also* Earmarking.)

COMMITMENT

A commitment is an administrative reservation of an allotment or of other funds in anticipation of their obligation. *(See also* Guaranteed Loan Commitment.)

COMMITTEE ALLOCATION

Amounts of spending recommended in the joint explanatory statement that accompanies the conference report on the congressional budget resolution and divided among the congressional committees according to their jurisdiction. House and Senate committees receive allocations of total new budget authority and total outlays. House committees also receive allocations of total entitlement authority and Senate committees also receive allocations of Social Security outlays.

For purposes of section 302(a) and 602(a) of the Congressional Budget and Impoundment Control Act of 1974 (2 U.S.C. 633 and 665a), an allocation is the distribution of total new budget authority, entitlement authority, and outlays to relevant committees based on the levels contained in a concurrent resolution on the budget. *(See also* Allocation.)

COMPARATIVE STATEMENT OF NEW BUDGET AUTHORITY

A table accompanying a regular or supplemental appropriations act in the report of the House or Senate Appropriations Committee. It compares the appropriation recommended for each account with the amount requested by the President and the amount enacted in the preceding fiscal year. In some cases, such as when a continuing appropriations act is considered, the statement may be inserted into the *Congressional Record. (See also* New Budget Authority.)

COMPOSITE OUTLAY RATE (BUDGET ENFORCEMENT ACT TERM)

The percent of new budget authority that is converted to outlays in the fiscal year for which the budget authority is provided and subsequent fiscal years, which is used to calculate the outlays associated with the special allowance for discretionary budget authority. The Budget Enforcement Act establishes the following rates: for the international category, 46 percent in the first year, 20 percent in the second year, 16 percent in the third year, and 8 percent in the fourth year; for the domestic category, 53 percent for the first year, 31 percent for the second year, 12 percent for the third year, and 2 percent for the fourth year. The BEA did not establish composite outlay rates for the defense category.

CONCURRENT RESOLUTION ON THE BUDGET

A resolution passed by both houses of the Congress, but not requiring the signature of the President, setting forth or revising the congressional budget for the concerning its adoption and set forth a procedure called "reconciliation" to assure congressional committee compliance with the concurrent resolution on the budget. (For a further discussion of the act, *see* appendix I. *See also* Committee Allocation; Concurrent Resolution on the Budget; Current Level Estimate; New Spending Authority; Reconciliation; Reconciliation Bill; Special Rules; Spending Authority. For terms relating to the Impoundment Control Act of 1974, *see* Deferral of Budget Authority; Expenditure; Impoundment.)

CONSTANT DOLLAR (ECONOMICS TERM)

A dollar value adjusted for changes in the average price level. A constant dollar is derived by dividing a current dollar amount by a price index. The resulting constant dollar value is that which would exist if prices had remained at the same average level as in the base period. Any changes in such constant dollar values would therefore reflect only changes in the real volume of goods and services, not changes in the price level. Constant dollar figures are commonly used to compute the real value of the gross domestic product and its components and to estimate the real level of federal receipts and outlays. (*See also* Current Dollar.)

CONSUMER PRICE INDEX (CPI) (ECONOMICS TERM)

A measure of the price level of a fixed "market basket" of goods and services relative to the value of that same basket in a designated base period. Measures for two population groups are currently published, CPI-U and CPI-W. CPI-U is based on a market basket determined by expenditure patterns of all urban households, while the market basket for CPI-W is determined by expenditure patterns of only urban wage-earner and clerical-worker families. The urban wage-earner and clerical-worker population consists of clerical workers, sales workers, craft workers, operatives, service workers, and laborers. Both indexes are published monthly by the Bureau of Labor Statistics. The CPI is used to adjust for inflation, the income payments of Social Security beneficiaries, and payments made by other programs.

CONTINGENT LIABILITY

An existing condition, situation, or set of circumstances which poses the possibility of a loss to an agency that will ultimately be resolved when one or more future events occur or fail to occur. Contingent liabilities may lead to outlays. Contingent liabilities arise, for example, with respect to unadjudicated claims and flood insurance, loan guarantee programs, and bank deposit insurance programs. Contingent liabilities are normally not covered by budget authority. However, under credit reform, for most programs, loan guarantee commitments cannot be made unless the Congress has made appropriations of budget authority to cover the credit subsidy cost in advance in annual appropriations acts. (*See also* Credit Subsidy Cost; Liability.)

COST

The payment for the possession, use, or accomplishment of an object or activity. It is the sacrifice incurred in economic activities—that which is given up or foregone to consume, to save, to exchange, to produce, and so forth. *(See also* Credit Subsidy Cost.)

COST-BENEFIT ANALYSIS
(ECONOMICS TERM)

An analytic technique that compares the costs and benefits of investments, programs, or policy actions in order to determine which alternative or alternatives maximize net benefits. Cost-benefit analysis attempts to consider all costs and benefits, regardless of whether they are reflected in market transactions. The costs and benefits included depend upon the scope of the analysis, for example, private or social, local, state, or national. Net benefits of an alternative are determined by subtracting the present value of costs from the present value of benefits. *(See also* Present Value. For a distinction, *see* Cost-Effectiveness Analysis.)

COST-EFFECTIVENESS ANALYSIS
(ECONOMICS TERM)

An analytic technique used to choose the most efficient method, that is, the lowest cost method, for achieving a given investment program or policy result. The scope of this analysis is more limited than that of cost-benefit analysis, which does not take the program or policy result as a given. (For a distinction, *see* Cost Benefit Analysis.)

COUNTERCYCLICAL POLICY
(ECONOMICS TERM)

Policy aimed at reducing the size and duration of swings in economic activity in order to keep economic growth closer to a pace consistent with low inflation and high employment. It includes monetary and fiscal policies affecting the level of interest rates, money supply, taxes, and government spending.

CREDIT BUDGET

The credit budget was the principal system of controlling the volume of federal credit prior to adoption of credit reform. It has now been superseded. Under the credit budget, the President's budget recommended limitations of the levels of total new direct loan obligations and total new guaranteed loan commitments, and the congressional budget resolutions included such limitations (which could differ from the President's recommendations). The budget resolution levels formed the basis for limitations on direct and guaranteed loans in appropriations acts. With the adoption of credit reform, the credit budget is no longer required, since the costs of new direct loans and loan guarantees are included directly in the budget.

CREDIT REFORM (BUDGET ENFORCEMENT ACT TERM)

The revised method of controlling and accounting for credit programs in the federal budget. The Federal Credit Reform Act of 1990 added Title V to the Congressional Budget Act of 1974. It requires that the net present value of the estimated long-term cost to the government of new direct loans and loan guarantees (the credit subsidy cost) be financed from new budget authority and be recorded as budget outlays at the time the direct or guaranteed loans are disbursed. In turn, it authorizes the creation of nonbudgetary financing accounts to receive this subsidy cost payment. *(See also* Budget Enforcement Act; Credit Subsidy Cost; Discount Rate; Present Value; Scorekeeping.)

CREDIT REESTIMATES

Recalculation of the estimated cost to the government of a group of direct loans or loan guarantees. After new direct loans or loan guarantees are made, the Federal Credit Reform Act requires periodic recalculations of the estimated (and, eventually, the actual) cost in order to determine the validity of the previous subsidy estimates and payments. All such recalculations are to be made in terms of the net present values applicable to the original loans or guarantees (with an associated recalculation of applicable cumulative interest). If any correction is determined to be required, the act requires that the correction (which could be additional subsidy and associated interest payments to, or refunds from, the financing accounts) be made, and provides permanent indefinite budget authority to finance the payments. The subsidy reestimates are required to be displayed as a distinct and separately identified subaccount in the credit program account.

CREDIT REFORM ACT ACCOUNTS

CREDIT PROGRAM ACCOUNT.

A budget account into which an appropriation to cover the subsidy cost (on a net present value basis) of a direct loan or loan guarantee program is made and from which such cost is disbursed to the financing account. Usually, a separate amount is also appropriated in the program account for administrative expenses that are directly related to credit program operations. (*See also* Present Value.)

FINANCING ACCOUNT.

A non-budget account (or accounts) associated with each credit program account which holds balances, receives the subsidy cost payment from the credit program account, and includes all other cash flows to and from the government resulting from direct loan obligations or loan guarantee commitments made on or after October 1, 1991.

LIQUIDATING ACCOUNT.

A budget account that includes all cash flows to and from the government resulting from direct loan obligations or loan guarantee commitments made prior to October 1,1991. The Federal Credit Reform Act of 1990 requires that such accounts be shown in the budget on a cash basis.

CREDIT SUBSIDY COST

The estimated long-term cost to the government of a direct loan or loan guarantee, calculated on a net present value basis, and excluding administrative costs. The Federal Credit Reform Act of 1990 specifies that, for direct loans, the credit subsidy cost is the net present value, at the time the loan is disbursed, of the following cash flows: (1) loan disbursements, (2) repayments of principal, and (3) payments of interest and other payments by or to the government over the life of the loan after adjusting for estimated defaults, prepayments, fees, penalties, and other recoveries. For loan guarantees, the act specifies that the credit subsidy cost is the net present value, at the time a guaranteed loan is disbursed by the lender, of the following cash flows: (1) estimated payments by the government to cover defaults, delinquencies, interest subsidies, or other payments and (2) the estimated payments to the government including origination and other fees, penalties, and recoveries. In estimating net present values, the discount rate is the average interest rate on marketable Treasury securities of similar maturity to the direct loan or loan guarantee for which the estimate is being made. (*See also* Credit Reform; Direct Loan; Guaranteed Loan; Present Value; Subsidy.)

CURRENT (BUDGET ENFORCEMENT ACT TERM)

With respect to OMB estimates, those consistent with economic and technical assumptions underlying the President's most recent annual budget submitted to the Congress. (For a distinction, *see* Up-to-Date.)

CURRENT DOLLAR (ECONOMICS TERM)

The dollar value of a good or service in terms of prices current at the time the good or service is sold. This contrasts with the value of the goods or services measured in constant dollars. (*See also* Constant Dollar.)

CURRENT LEVEL ESTIMATE

An estimate of the amounts of new budget authority, outlays, and revenues for a full fiscal year, based upon enacted law. Current level estimates used by the Congress do not take into account the potential effects of pending legislation. Current level estimates include a tabulation comparing estimates with the aggregates approved in the most recent budget resolution. Section 308(b) of the Congressional Budget and Impoundment Control Act of 1974, as amended, (2 U.S.C. 639(b)), requires the respective Budget Committees to make this tabulation at least once a month. The Congressional Budget Office assists these committees by submitting reports on a regular basis of the budgetary impact of congressional actions. (*See also* Budget

Authority; Committee Allocation; Congressional Budget Act; Scorekeeping.)

CURRENT SERVICES ESTIMATES

Estimates submitted by the President of the levels of budget authority and outlays for the ensuing fiscal year based on the continuation of existing levels of service. These estimates reflect the anticipated costs of continuing federal programs and activities at present levels without policy changes. Such estimates ignore all new presidential or congressional initiatives, including reductions, that are not yet law.

With his proposed budget each year, the President must transmit current services estimates and the economic assumptions upon which they are based. Current services estimates are also included in the "Mid-Session Review of the Budget," but are not identified by that title, and are confined to those programs that are essentially automatic (that is, they exclude programs controlled through annual appropriations). The current services data in the Mid-Session Review are identified as being for "mandatory and related programs under current law."

The Congressional Budget Office also prepares similar estimates. (For a more detailed discussion of this term, *see* "Baseline Estimates" in the *Budget of the United States Government. See also* Baseline; Multiyear Budget Planning.)

CURRENT YEAR

See under Fiscal Year

DEBT, FEDERAL

There are three basic tabulations of federal debt: (1) gross federal debt, (2) debt held by the public, and (3) debt subject to statutory limit. *(See also* Borrowing Authority *under* Budget Authority; Means of Financing.)

GROSS FEDERAL DEBT

All federal government debt securities outstanding, whether issued by Treasury or by other agencies and whether held by the public or by government accounts. Gross federal debt is categorized as debt issued by the Department of Treasury or by other agencies.

Treasury Debt/Public Debt.

That portion of the gross federal debt issued by Treasury (which includes the Federal Financing Bank (FFB)) to the public or another fund or account. To avoid double counting, FFB borrowing from Treasury is not included in Treasury debt. Treasury debt has also been called "public debt" but is not the same as "debt held by the public."

Agency Debt.

That portion of the gross federal debt incurred when a federal agency other than Treasury is authorized by law to issue debt securities directly to the public or another fund or account. Since Treasury or FFB borrowing required to obtain the money to lend to the agency is already part of the gross federal debt, to avoid double counting, agency borrowing from Treasury or the FFB and federal fund advances to trust funds are not included in the gross federal debt. Debt of government-sponsored, privately owned enterprises, such as the Federal National Mortgage Association, is not included in the federal debt.

Debt Held by the Public

That part of the gross federal debt held outside of the federal government. This includes any federal debt held by individuals, corporations, state or local governments, the Federal Reserve System, and foreign governments and central banks. Debt held by government trust funds, revolving funds, and special funds is excluded from debt held by the public. Debt held by the public is distinct from public debt or Treasury debt.

Debt Subject to Statutory Limit

As defined by the Second Liberty Bond Act of 1917, as amended, it includes virtually all Treasury debt. However, only a small portion of agency debt is included in this tabulation of federal debt. The Tennessee Valley Authority is an example of an entity whose debt is not subject to the statutory limitation on the federal debt. Debt subject to statutory limit is a broader category than debt held by the public. (For an explanation of "limit," *see* Limitation.)

The Rules of the House of Representatives provide that whenever the House adopts a budget resolution that includes an increase in the public debt limit, the House automatically passes a joint resolution increasing the statutory limit.

DEBT SERVICE

Payment of interest on and repayment of principal on borrowed funds. The term may also be used to refer to payment of interest alone. (*See also* Means of Financing.)

DEFERRAL OF BUDGET AUTHORITY

Temporary withholding or delaying the obligation or expenditure of budget authority or any other type of executive action which effectively precludes the obligation or expenditure of budget authority. Budget authority may be deferred to provide for contingencies, to achieve savings or greater efficiency in the operations of the government, or as otherwise specifically provided by law. Budget authority may not be deferred in order to effect a policy in lieu of one established by law or for any other reason.

Deferrals may be proposed by agencies but must be communicated to the Congress by the President in a special message. Deferred budget authority may not be withheld from obligation unless an act is passed to approve the deferral and the act is presented to the President. Additionally, unless the Congress has approved a deferral, budget authority whose availability expires at the end of the fiscal year must be made available with sufficient time remaining in the fiscal year to obligate that budget authority before the end of the fiscal year. (*See also* Apportionment; Budgetary Reserves; Impoundment; Rescission.)

DEFICIENCY APPORTIONMENT

An apportionment by the Office of Management and Budget for the fiscal year in an amount or rate that may compel the enactment of supplemental budget authority. Such apportionments may only be made under certain specified conditions as provided for in the Antideficiency Act, 31 U.S.C. 1515. In such instances, the need for additional budget authority is usually indicated by apportioning for the fourth quarter less than the amount that will actually be required. Approval of

requests for deficiency apportionment does not authorize agencies to
exceed available resources within an account. *(See also* Antideficiency
Act; Apportionment; Deficiency Appropriation; Supplemental
Appropriation.)

DEFICIENCY APPROPRIATION

A type of supplemental appropriation which provides budget
authority necessary to cover obligations that have been incurred in
excess of available authority.

DEFICIT

BUDGET DEFICIT

The amount by which the government's budget outlays exceed
its budget receipts for a given period, usually a fiscal year. For
purposes of defining deficits under Gramm-Rudman-Hollings as amended
by the Budget Enforcement Act, this amount excludes the off-budget
activities such as the outlays and receipts of the Postal Service and
Social Security. *(See also* Budget Surplus *under* Surplus.)

TOTAL DEFICIT

The amount by which the government's on-budget and off-budget
outlays exceed the sum of its on-budget and off-budget receipts for a
given period, usually a fiscal year. *(See also* Budget Surplus *under*
Surplus; Off-Budget Federal Entity.)

DEFLATION (ECONOMICS TERM)

A sustained decrease in the general price level.

DEFLATOR (ECONOMICS TERM)

An index used to adjust a current dollar amount to its constant
dollar counterpart, that is, to remove the effects of inflation.

DEOBLIGATION

An agency's cancellation or downward adjustment of previously recorded obligations.

DEPRECIATION

The allocation of the costs, less salvage value, of fixed assets, including equipment, buildings, and other structures, over their useful lives in a systematic and rational manner. Depreciation reflects the use of the asset(s) during specific operating periods in order to match costs with related revenues in measuring income or determining the costs of carrying out program activities.

DIRECT LOAN

A disbursement of funds by the government to a nonfederal borrower under a contract that requires the repayment of such funds with or without interest. The term includes the purchase of, or the participation in, a loan made by a nonfederal lender. It also includes the sale of a government asset on credit terms of more than 90 days duration. It does not include the acquisition of federally guaranteed nonfederal loans in the satisfaction of default or other guarantee loan claims or the price support loans of the Commodity Credit Corporation. Under credit reform, the budget records the credit subsidy cost of direct loans as outlays. The subsidies are paid to the direct loan financing accounts which, in turn, make the loans to the public. (For more information, *see* the discussion, "Technical Perspectives on Expenditures, Off-Budget Activities, Capital Outlays, and Borrowing," and the table, "Guaranteed Loan Transactions of the Federal Government," in the *Budget of the United States Government. See also* Asset Sale/Loan Prepayment; Credit Reform; Credit Subsidy Cost; Direct Loan Obligation; Guaranteed Loan.)

DIRECT LOAN OBLIGATION

A binding agreement by a federal agency to make a direct loan when specified conditions are fulfilled by the borrower.

Under credit reform, direct loan obligations are composed of obligations for both the credit subsidy cost and the unsubsidized amounts of the loan. When an agency enters into a direct loan obligation, it obligates itself to pay the credit subsidy cost to the direct loan financing account and the financing account is committed to make the loan to the borrower. Only the credit subsidy cost is recorded as a budgetary obligation. (For a more detailed discussion, *see* "Recognizing Federal Underwriting Risks" in the *Budget of the United States Government. See also* Direct Loan.)

DIRECT SPENDING AUTHORITY (BUDGET ENFORCEMENT ACT TERM)

Entitlement authority, the Food Stamp Program, and budget authority provided by law other than appropriations acts. Direct spending authority is under the control of the authorizing committees as contrasted with discretionary spending under the control of the appropriations committees that is controlled year-to-year in the appropriations process. From the perspective of the appropriations process, direct spending is mandatory (not controllable through appropriations). New direct spending is subject to pay-as-you-go requirements. *(See also* Entitlement Authority; Mandatory; Pay-As-You-Go; Spending Authority. For a distinction, *see* Discretionary Appropriations.)

DISCOUNT RATE (ECONOMICS TERM)

One of the following:

(1) The interest rate that a commercial bank pays when it borrows from a Federal Reserve bank. The discount rate is one of the tools of monetary policy used by the Federal Reserve System. The Federal Reserve customarily raises or lowers the discount rate to signal a shift toward restraining or easing its money and credit policy. *(See also* Monetary Policy.)

(2) The interest rate used to determine the present value of a future stream of receipts and outlays, or in cost-benefit analysis, of benefits and costs. This use of the term is completely distinct from that in monetary policy, and the interest rates involved are generally not those charged by Federal Reserve banks.

Discount rate policies of the three major oversight and budget agencies—GAO, OMB, and CBO—are consistent with basic economic principles but vary significantly in their formulations for different analyses. *Discount Rate Policy* (GAO/ OCE-17. 1.1), May 1991, describes the different policies and their applications. (3) In estimating net present values under credit reform, the average interest rate on marketable Treasury securities of similar maturity to the direct loan or loan guarantee for which the estimate is being made.

DISCRETIONARY

A term that usually modifies either "spending," "appropriation," or "amount." "Discretionary spending" refers to outlays controllable through the congressional appropriation process. The Budget Enforcement Act uses the term "discretionary appropriations" to refer to budgetary resources (except to fund direct-spending programs) provided in appropriations acts. (*See also* Appropriation Act; Appropriations and One-Year (Annual) Authority *under* Budget Authority; Gramm-Rudman-Hollings. For a contrast, *see* Entitlement Authority; Mandatory.)

DISCRETIONARY APPROPRIATIONS (BUDGET ENFORCEMENT ACT TERM)

Budgetary resources (except to fund direct spending programs) provided in appropriation acts. The Budget Enforcement Act sets forth spending limitations or caps for discretionary appropriations. (*See also* Appropriations *under* Budget Authority; Baseline; Direct Spending; Discretionary; Discretionary Spending Limits; Mandatory.)

DISCRETIONARY SPENDING LIMITS/SPENDING CAPS (BUDGET ENFORCEMENT ACT TERM)

Under the Budget Enforcement Act (BEA), maximum amounts of new budget authority and outlays for specific categories of discretionary appropriations. For fiscal years 1991,1992, and 1993, BEA limits new budget authority and outlays in three separate categories of discretionary appropriations—defense, international, and domestic. Discretionary appropriations included within each category are so designated in the joint explanatory statements of managers accompanying the conference report on the Omnibus Budget Reconciliation Act of 1990. For fiscal year 1994 and 1995, BEA limits new budget authority and outlays for a single category—total discretionary appropriations. If appropriations are enacted that cause discretionary spending to exceed the limits within a particular

category, a sequestration will occur—within the applicable category—
to eliminate the amount of the excess.

BEA requires the President to adjust the discretionary spending
limits for specific reasons. These reasons are:

(1) changes in concepts and definitions,
(2) changes in inflation,
(3) reestimates of the costs of credit programs,
(4) increased funding for the IRS compliance initiative,
(5) debt forgiveness for Poland and Egypt,
(6) additional funding for the International Monetary Fund,
(7) designated emergency appropriations,
(8) special allowances for certain excess amounts of new budget
    authority, and
(9) special allowances for certain excess amounts of outlays.

EARMARKING

Either of the following:

(1) Dedicating collections by law for a specific purpose or program.
    Earmarked collections comprise trust fund receipt accounts,
    special fund receipt accounts, and offsetting collections credited
    to appropriation accounts. These collections may be classified as
    budget receipts, proprietary receipts, or reimbursements to
    appropriations.
(2) Dedicating appropriations for a particular purpose. Legislative
    language may designate any portion of a lump-sum amount for
    particular purposes. *(See also* Special Fund Accounts and Trust
    Fund Accounts *under* Account in the President's Budget;
    Offsetting Collections and Proprietary Receipts *under*
    Collections; Committee Allocation.)

EMERGENCY APPROPRIATION (BUDGET ENFORCEMENT ACT TERM)

For fiscal years 1991 through 1995, an appropriation designated
as an emergency requirement by both the President and the Congress.
Under BEA, the discretionary spending limits are adjusted by the total
amount of such appropriations for the fiscal year in which the
appropriation was enacted and each succeeding year through 1995 and
will not cause a sequestration. *(See also* Appropriations *under* Budget
Authority.)

EMERGENCY LEGISLATION (BUDGET ENFORCEMENT ACT TERM)

For fiscal years 1991 through 1995, a provision of direct spending or receipts legislation designated as an emergency requirement by the both the President and the Congress. Under BEA, such legislation is not subject to the pay-as-you-go requirements and will not cause a sequestration. (See also Adjustments to Discretionary Spending Limits; Direct Spending; Discretionary.)

ENTITLEMENT AUTHORITY

Authority to make payments (including loans and grants) for which budget authority is not provided in advance by appropriation acts to any person or government if, under the provisions of the law containing such authority, the U.S. government is obligated to make the payments to persons or governments who meet the requirements established by law (2 U.S.C. 622(9), 651(c)(2)(C)).

Under the Budget Enforcement Act, new entitlement authority is considered direct spending and subject to the pay-as-you-go provisions. (See also Appropriated Entitlement; Authorizing Legislation; Backdoor Authority/Backdoor Spending; Budget Enforcement Act; Mandatory; Pay-As-You-Go; Spending Authority.)

EXCESS DEFICIT (BUDGET ENFORCEMENT ACT TERM)

The amount by which the estimated deficit for the budget year exceeds the sum of the following: the maximum deficit amount for that year, any emergency direct spending or receipts, and--if there is not a full adjustment for technical and economic reestimates--deposit insurance reestimates. For fiscal years 1992 and 1993, the margin is zero; therefore, any excess deficit triggers sequestration. However, if the discretionary spending limits and the pay-as-you-go requirement for direct spending are met, the maximum deficit amount should not be exceeded through fiscal year 1993. For fiscal years 1994 and 1995, any excess deficit greater than the $15 billion margin triggers sequestration. (See also Direct Spending Authority; Discretionary Spending Limits; Emergency Legislation; Margin; Maximum Deficit Amount; Sequestration.)

EXEMPT PROGRAMS AND ACTIVITIES
(BUDGET ENFORCEMENT ACT TERM)

A list of programs contained in Section 255 of Gramm-Rudman-Hollings, as amended by the Budget Enforcement Act (2 U.S.C. 905) that are not subject to sequestration. The major exempt programs are Social Security, certain railroad retirement benefits, net interest, certain low-income programs, veterans' compensation and pensions, and offsetting receipts and collections. Except as specified (2 U.S.C. 906), administrative expense components of exempt accounts are subject to sequestration. Unobligated balances of budget authority carried over from prior fiscal years, except balances in the defense category, are exempt from reduction under any sequestration order. The President may, with respect to a military personnel account, exempt that account or provide for a lower uniform percentage reduction than would otherwise apply. However, the President must notify the Congress of how this authority will be exercised on or before August 10 of the budget year. If the President invokes this authority, the sequestration applicable to the remainder of defense must make up the difference, so that the total defense sequestration is unchanged. *(See also* Budgetary Resources; Gramm-Rudman-Hollings; Sequestrable Resource; Uniform Reduction Percentage.)

EXPENDED APPROPRIATIONS

Charges during a given period that reflect the costs incurred and the need to pay for (1) services performed by employees, contractors, vendors, carriers, grantees, lessors, and other payees, (2) goods and other tangible property received and accepted, and (3) amounts to be owed in the future under programs for which no current service or performance is required, such as annuities, insurance claims, other benefit payments, and some cash grants. Expended appropriations exclude the repayment of debt, which is considered neither an obligation nor an expenditure and accrue regardless of when cash payments are made, whether invoices have been rendered, or, in some cases, whether goods or other tangible property have been physically delivered. This term was formerly known as "Accrued Expenditures." *(See also* Accrual Basis *under* Bases of Budgeting; Expenditure; Liability.)

EXPENDITURE

With respect to provisions of the Antideficiency Act (31 U.S.C. 1513-1514) and the Congressional Budget and Impoundment Control Act of 1974 (2 U.S.C. 622(i)), a term that has the same definition as outlay. *(See also* Antideficiency Act; Antideficiency Act Violation; Congressional Budget Act; Outlay. For a distinction, *see* Accrued Expenditure.)

EXPENSE

For accounting purposes, the outflow of assets or incurrence of liabilities (or both) during a period as a result of rendering services, delivering or producing goods, or carrying out other normal operating activities.

EXPIRED ACCOUNT

An appropriation or fund account in which the balance is no longer available for incurring new obligations because the time available for incurring such obligations has expired. Expired accounts will be maintained by fiscal year identity for 5 years. During this 5-year period, obligations may be adjusted if otherwise proper and outlays may be made from these accounts. Unobligated balances will not be withdrawn from expired accounts. They will remain available for legitimate obligation adjustments or for obligations properly chargeable to such accounts, which should have been but were not recorded, but not for new obligations. After the five-year period has elapsed, all obligated and unobligated balances are canceled and the expired account is closed.

FEED AND FORAGE ACT

The source of legal authority for the Department of Defense and the Coast Guard (when acting under the Navy's command) to contract or purchase "clothing, subsistence, forage, fuel, quarters, transportation, or medical and hospital supplies" in excess of amounts otherwise authorized by law.

FEEDER ACCOUNT

Appropriation and revolving fund accounts whose resources are available only for transfer to other appropriation or revolving fund accounts.

FINANCING ACCOUNT

See under Credit Reform Act Accounts *under* Credit Reform

FINANCING TRANCHE

All of the direct loans or guaranteed loans within a cohort, separately identified by risk category, that are disbursed in the same quarter and that have similar maturity. *(See also* Cohort; Credit Reform; Direct Loan; Guaranteed Loan.)

FISCAL POLICY

Federal government policies with respect to taxes and spending which are intended to promote the nation's macroeconomic goals, particularly with respect to employment, gross domestic product, price level stability, equilibrium in the balance of payments, the exchange rate, the current account, and the national savings/investment balance. The budget process is a major vehicle for determining and implementing federal fiscal policy. *(See also* Monetary Policy.)

FISCAL YEAR

Any yearly accounting period, regardless of its relationship to a calendar year. The fiscal year for the federal government begins on October 1 of each year and ends on September 30 of the following year; it is designated by the calendar year in which it ends. For example, fiscal year 1990 began October 1,1989, and ended September 30, 1990. (Prior to fiscal year 1977, the federal fiscal year began on July 1 and ended on June 30.)

BUDGET YEAR

The fiscal year for which the budget is being considered, that is the fiscal year following the current year. For Budget Enforcement Act purposes, the term budget year means, with respect to a session of Congress, the fiscal year of the Government that starts on October 1 of the calendar year in which that session begins.

CURRENT YEAR

The fiscal year immediately preceding the budget year. For Budget Enforcement Act purposes, the term current year means, with respect to a budget year, the fiscal year that immediately precedes that budget year.

PRIOR YEAR

The fiscal year immediately preceding the current year.

FIXED APPROPRIATION ACCOUNT

An account in which appropriations are available for obligation for a definite period of time. A fixed appropriation account can receive appropriations available for obligation for one year (an annual account) or for a specified number of years (a multiyear account). (For a distinction, *see* No-Year Authority *under* Duration *under* Budget Authority.)

FULL FUNDING

The provision of budgetary resources to cover the total estimated cost of a program or project at the time it is undertaken (regardless of when the funds will actually be obligated).

Full funding generally pertains to multiyear activities, such as the construction of Navy ships, whether or not all of the funds are obligated in the first year. It differs from partial funding under which budgetary resources are provided annually only for the amount expected to be obligated during that year. (For a distinction, *see* Incremental

Funding. *See also* Multiple-Year Authority *under* Duration *under* Budget Authority; Multiyear Budget Planning.)

The term full funding sometimes refers to the appropriation of the total amount authorized by law. A program is said to be fully funded when the appropriation equals the authorized level or when appropriations are sufficient to cover service for all eligible persons or organizations.

FUNCTIONAL CLASSIFICATION

A system of classifying budget resources so that budget authority, outlays, receipts, and tax expenditures can be related to the national needs being addressed. Each concurrent resolution on the budget allocates these budgetary resources— except receipts and tax expenditures—among the various functions in the budget.

Each budget account is generally placed in the single budget function (for example, national defense or health) that best reflects its major purpose, an important national need. A function may be divided into two or more subfunctions, depending upon the complexity of the national need addressed. *(See also* Budget Activity; National Needs.)

(For a presentation of the functional classification for the fiscal 1993 budget, *see* appendix II. For a distinction, *see* Object Classification. *See also* Agency Mission; Budget Activity; Mission Budgeting; National Needs; Subfunction.)

FUND ACCOUNTING

The legal requirement that federal agencies establish accounts for segregating revenues, other resources, related liabilities, obligations, and balances in order to carry out specific activities or achieve certain objectives in accordance with special regulations, restrictions, or limitations. In a broad sense, the federal government requires fund accounting to demonstrate agency compliance with existing legislation for which government funds have been appropriated or otherwise authorized.

One of the most important laws requiring federal agencies to adhere to fund accounting concepts is the Antideficiency Act. *(See also* Antideficiency Act.)

GOVERNMENT-SPONSORED ENTERPRISE (GSE)

A privately owned and operated federally chartered financial institution that facilitates the flow of investment funds to specific economic sectors. GSEs, acting as financial intermediaries, provide these sectors access to national capital markets. The activities of GSEs are not included in the federal budget's totals because they are classified as private entities. However, because of their relationship to the government, detailed statements of financial operations and condition are presented as supplementary information in the budget document. For the purposes of the Congressional Budget Act of 1974, as amended (2 U.S.C. 622(8)), an entity must meet certain criteria to qualify as a GSE. (For distinctions, *see* Mixed-Ownership Government Corporation; Off-Budget Federal Entity; Wholly Owned Government Corporation.)

GRAMM-RUDMAN-HOLLINGS (GRH)

The names of the Senate sponsors (Senators Phil Gramm, Warren Rudman, and Ernest F. Hollings) of the original legislation and the common name for the Balanced Budget and Emergency Deficit Control Act of 1985, as amended most recently by the Budget Enforcement Act of 1990 (2 U.S.C. 900-922). The original GRH set declining deficit targets and specified automatic deficit reduction procedures. These procedures were substantially revised by the Budget Enforcement Act. *(See also* Automatic Spending Increase; Budget Enforcement Act; Discretionary; Exempt Programs and Activities; Limitation; Mandatory; Maximum Deficit Amount; Sequestrable Resource; Sequestration.)

GRANT

A federal financial assistance award making payment in cash or in kind for a specified purpose. The federal government is not expected to have substantial involvement with the state or local government or other recipient while the contemplated activity is being performed. The term "grants" frequently has a broader meaning and may include grants to nongovernmental recipients, whereas the term "grants-in-aid" is commonly restricted to grants to states and local governments. *(See* the Federal Grant and Cooperative Agreement Act of

1977, 31 U.S.C. 6301-6308.) The two major forms of federal grants-in-aid are block and categorical.

Block grants are given primarily to general purpose governmental units in accordance with a statutory formula. Such grants can be used for a variety of activities within a broad functional area. Examples of federal block-grant programs are the Omnibus Crime Control and Safe Streets Act of 1968, the Housing and Community Development Act of 1974, and the grants to states for social services under Title XX of the Social Security Act.

Categorical grants can be used only for a specific program. They may be formula or project grants. Formula grants allocate federal funds to states or their subdivisions in accordance with a distribution formula prescribed by law or administrative regulation. Project grants provide federal funding for fixed or known periods for specific projects or the delivery of specific services or products.

GROSS DOMESTIC PRODUCT (GDP) (ECONOMICS TERM)

The value of all final goods and services produced within the borders of the United States in a given period of time, whether produced by residents or nonresidents. (See also Gross National Product; National Income and Product Accounts.)

GROSS NATIONAL PRODUCT (GNP) (ECONOMICS TERM)

The value of all final goods and services produced by labor and capital supplied by residents of the United States in a given period of time, whether or not the residents are located within the United States. Depreciation charges and other allowances for business and institutional consumption of fixed capital goods are subtracted from GNP to derive net national product. GNP is the sum of the purchases of final goods and services by persons and governments, gross private domestic investment (including the change in business inventories), and net exports (exports less imports). The GNP can be expressed in current or constant dollars. (See also Gross Domestic Product; National Income and Product Accounts.)

GUARANTEED LOAN

A nonfederal loan to which a federal guarantee is attached. The loan principal is recorded as a guaranteed loan regardless of whether the federal guarantee is full or partial. For the purposes of the Federal Credit Reform Act (2 U.S.C. 661-661(f), a loan guarantee is defined as any guarantee, insurance, or other pledge with respect to the payment of all or a part of the principal or interest on any debt obligation of a nonfederal borrower to a nonfederal lender, but does not include the insurance of deposits, shares, or other withdrawable accounts in financial institutions. *(See also* Credit Reform; Direct Loan; Guaranteed Loan Commitment.)

GUARANTEED LOAN COMMITMENT

A binding agreement by a federal agency to make a loan guarantee when specified conditions are fulfilled by the borrower, the lender, or any other party to the guarantee agreement. *(See also* Commitment; Credit Reform; Guaranteed Loan.)

HIGH EMPLOYMENT BUDGET (ECONOMICS TERM)

The estimated receipts, outlays, and surplus or deficit that would occur if the U.S. economy were operating at a specified low level of unemployment (traditionally defined as a certain unemployment rate of the civilian labor force). *(See also* Structural Deficit.)

IDENTIFICATION CODE

Each appropriation or fund account in the *Budget of the United States Government* carries an 1 1-digit code that identifies (1) the agency, (2) the account, (3) the timing of the transmittal to the Congress, (4) the type of fund, and (5) the account's functional and subfunctional classifications. (For a detailed explanation of the account identification code, *see* appendix III.)

IMPLICIT PRICE DEFLATOR (GDP DEFLATOR) (ECONOMICS TERM)

For a particular year, the ratio of the gross domestic product's (GDP) current dollar value to its constant dollar value. The deflator is implicit because the constant dollar value for total GDP is calculated independently (as the sum of parts that have been individually adjusted to constant dollar terms). For this reason, the value of the deflator is affected by shifts in current dollar expenditure patterns among categories.

IMPOUNDMENT

Any action or inaction by an officer or employee of the federal government that precludes obligation or expenditure of budget authority. *(See also* Deferral of Budget Authority; Rescission.)

INCREMENTAL FUNDING

The provision or recording of budgetary resources for a program or project based on obligations estimated to be incurred within a fiscal year when such budgetary resources will not cover all the program's or project's obligations. Contracts that cannot be separated for performance by fiscal year may not be funded on an incremental basis without statutory authority. (For a distinction, *see* Full Funding.)

INFLATION (ECONOMICS TERM)

A sustained rise in the general price level.

INFLATOR

An index used to adjust a nominal dollar amount in one period to its nominal dollar counterpart in another, that is, to adjust the amount for the effects of inflation. *(See also* Adjustment for Changes in Inflation *under* Adjustments to Discretionary Spending Limits.)

INTERNAL CONTROL

Plan of organization, methods, and procedures adopted by management to ensure that (1) resource use is consistent with laws, regulations, and policies; (2) resources are safeguarded against waste, loss, and misuse; and (3) reliable data are obtained, maintained, and fairly disclosed in reports. *See also Assessing Internal Controls in Performance Audits* (GAO/OP-4. 1.4), September 1990.

JOINT RESOLUTION

Either of the following:

(1) A congressional action that becomes law in the same manner as a bill (that is, bicameral enactment and presentment to the President). While there is no real difference between a bill and a joint resolution, the latter is generally used in dealing with matters such as a single appropriation for a specific purpose. Joint resolutions are typically used to increase the statutory limit on the public debt and for continuing appropriations. These joint resolutions require a majority vote, just as bills do.

(2) A congressional action used to propose amendments to the Constitution. Resolutions to propose amendments to the Constitution are not presented to the President for approval. Adoption of a joint resolution to propose a constitutional amendment requires a two-thirds majority vote. An amendment proposed by a joint resolution becomes effective when ratified by three-fourths of the states.

(See also Continuing Appropriation *under* Budget Authority; Final Sequestration Report *under* Sequestration Reports. For a distinction, *see* Concurrent Resolution on the Budget.)

LIABILITY

Assets owed for items received, services received, assets acquired, construction performed (regardless of whether invoices have been received), an amount received but not yet earned, or other expenses incurred.

Liabilities include (1) amounts owed for goods in the hands of contractors under the constructive delivery concept (when an agency, the seller, meets long-term contract obligations) and (2) amounts owed under grants, pensions, awards, and other indebtedness not involving the furnishing of goods and services. *(See also* Accrued Expenditure; Asset; Contingent Liability.)

LIMITATION

A restriction on the amount of budgetary resources that can be obligated or committed for a specific purpose. While limitations are most often established through appropriations acts, they can also be established through authorizing legislation. Limitations may be placed on the availability of funds for program levels, administrative expenses, direct loan obligations, guaranteed loan commitments, or other purposes. For the purposes of the Budget Enforcement Act, obligation limitations are one type of budgetary resource because they establish the amount that can be obligated. *(See also* Administrative Division or Subdivision of Funds; Apportionment; Appropriation Act; Authorizing Legislation; Gramm-Rudman-Hollings; Duration and Extensions of Budget Authority *under* Budget Authority.)

LINE ITEM

In executive budgeting, a particular expenditure, such as program, subprogram, or travel costs and equipment. In congressional budgeting, it usually refers to assumptions about particular programs or accounts implicit but not explicit in the budget resolution. In appropriations acts, it usually refers to an individual account or part of an account for which a specific amount is available. *(See also* Line-Item Veto; Mission Budgeting; Obligated Balance *under* Obligational Authority.)

LINE-ITEM VETO

A power (not presently granted to the President) to disapprove—in the same manner allowed under article I, section 7 of the Constitution—one or both of the following:

(1) particular items of expenditures or
(2) budget accounts indicated in the budget.

Granting the President a line-item veto would require a constitutional change or a series of legislative and statutory changes. The line-item veto exists at the state level in forms that vary from state to state. *(See also* Account in Treasury's Annual Report Appendix; Line Item.)

LIQUIDATING ACCOUNT

See under Credit Reform Act Accounts *under* Credit Reform

LOOK-BACK (BUDGET ENFORCEMENT ACT TERM)

Two Budget Enforcement Act procedures governing sequestration. One applies to Discretionary Appropriations and the other to Direct Spending.

- If, after June 30, a discretionary appropriation for the fiscal year in progress causes a breach within a category for that year (after taking into account any sequestration of amounts within that category), the discretionary spending limits for that category for the next fiscal year must be reduced by the amount of the breach.
- Within 15 days after the Congress adjourns, there must be a sequestration to offset any net deficit increase in that fiscal year and the prior fiscal year caused by all direct spending and receipts legislation enacted after the enactment of the Budget Enforcement Act (after adjusting for any prior sequestration). Such an end-of-session sequestration is termed a look-back sequestration. *(See also* Breach; Category of Discretionary Spending; Discretionary Spending Sequestration and Pay-As-You-Go Sequestration *under* Sequestration; Pay-As-You-Go Sequestration Report *under* Sequestration Reports; Sequestration.)

LOW-GROWTH REPORT (BUDGET ENFORCEMENT ACT TERM)

A notification to the Congress by CBO that (1) either CBO or OMB estimates or projects two consecutive quarters of negative real economic growth during the current quarter, the preceding quarter, and the following four quarters, or (2) during the most recently reported quarter and the immediately preceding quarter, the Department of Commerce's report of actual real economic growth indicates economic growth of less than one percent. The Congress may consider suspending sequestration procedures in the event of a low-growth report. *(See also* Real Economic Growth; Suspension of Sequestration Procedures.)

M ACCOUNT

A successor account into which obligated balances (unexpended funds) under an appropriation were transferred from the expired account (merged) at the end of the second full fiscal year following expiration. The National Defense Authorization Act of 1991 (Public Law 101-510) amended the procedures for closing appropriation and fund accounts. Under this legislation, no new M accounts will be established and existing M accounts will be phased out. (For a discussion of the new procedures for closing accounts, *see* Expired Account. *See also* Merged Surplus Account.)

MANDATORY

A term that usually modifies either "spending," "amount," or "appropriation." "Mandatory spending" refers to outlays for entitlement programs such as food stamps, Medicare, veterans' pensions, payment of interest on the public debt, and nonentitlements such as payments to states from Forest Service receipts. By defining eligibility and setting the benefit or payment rules, the Congress controls spending for these programs indirectly rather than directly through the appropriations process. "Mandatory amount" is used in the Congressional Budget Act, as modified by Gramm-Rudman-Hollings, as a synonym for "relatively uncontrollable." "Relatively uncontrollable" generally means budget authority or budget outlays that the Congress and the President cannot increase or decrease in a given year without changing existing substantive law. *(See also* Appropriations, Multiple-Year Authority, and No-Year Authority *under* Budget Authority; Committee Allocation; Direct Spending Authority; Discretionary; Entitlement Authority; Gramm-Rudman-Hollings.)

For purposes of Part C of the Balanced Budget and Emergency Deficit Control Act of 1985 (GRH), as amended by the Budget Enforcement Act, entitlement authority includes the list of mandatory appropriations included in the joint explanatory statement of managers accompanying the conference report on the Omnibus Budget Reconciliation Act of 1990.

MARGIN (BUDGET ENFORCEMENT ACT TERM)

The amount by which the deficit may exceed the maximum deficit amount for the year without triggering sequestration. The margin for fiscal years 1992 and 1993 is zero and for fiscal years 1994 and 1995 is $15 billion. *(See also* Excess Deficit; Maximum Deficit Amount; Sequestration.)

MAXIMUM DEFICIT AMOUNT (BUDGET ENFORCEMENT ACT TERM)

The targeted limit for a fiscal year deficit as specified under Title VI of the Congressional Budget Act, as amended. The Budget Enforcement Act requires specified adjustments to the maximum deficit amount and permits the President to make optional adjustments for economic and technical reasons for fiscal years 1994 and 1995. *(See also* Adjustments to Maximum Deficit Amount; Gramm-Rudman-Hollings; Margin; Sequestration.)

MEANS OF FINANCING

Ways in which a budget deficit is financed or a budget surplus is used. A budget deficit may be financed by Treasury (or agency) borrowing, by reducing Treasury cash balances, by the sale of gold, by seigniorage, by allowing certain unpaid liabilities to increase, or by other similar transactions. Some means of increasing Treasury cash balances, however, can add to the financing requirements of government. A budget surplus may be used to repay borrowing or to build up cash balances. *(See also* Debt, Federal; Debt Service; Seigniorage.)

MERGED SURPLUS ACCOUNT

An account that represented an unobligated balance from an appropriation whose period of availability had been expired for more than 2 years. The National Defense Authorization Act of 1991 (Public Law 101-510) amended the procedures for closing appropriation and fund accounts. Under this legislation, no new merged surplus accounts will be established and existing ones will be phased out. *(See also* Expired Account; M Account.)

MIDSESSION REVIEW OF THE BUDGET

A supplemental summary to the budget the President submits to the Congress in January or February of that year. As required by 31

U.S.C. 1106, the midsession review contains revised estimates of budget receipts, outlays, and budget authority and other summary information. OMB is required to issue it by July 15 of each year.

MISSION BUDGETING

A budget approach that focuses on purpose rather than input and directs attention to an agency's success in meeting its responsibilities. By grouping programs and activities according to an agency's mission or end purposes, mission budgeting makes it easier to identify similar programs. At the highest level in the budget structure, mission represents basic end-purpose responsibilities assigned to an agency. Descending levels in the budget structure then focus more sharply on the specific components of the mission and the programs needed to satisfy it. Line items, the supporting activities necessary to satisfy the mission, are at the lowest levels in the budget structure. *(See also* Agency Mission; Functional Classification; Line Item.)

MIXED-OWNERSHIP GOVERNMENT CORPORATION

An enterprise or business activity established by statute and designated by the Government Corporation Control Act (31 U.S.C. 9101), as a mixed-ownership government corporation. The fiscal activities of some mixed-ownership government corporations appear in the budget. The Rural Telephone Bank is an example of such a corporation. *(See also* Government-Sponsored Enterprise; Off-Budget Federal Entity; Wholly-Owned Government Corporation.)

MONETARY POLICY (ECONOMICS TERM)

Policies directly affecting the money supply, interest rates, and credit availability that are intended to promote national macroeconomic goals, particularly goals concerning employment, gross domestic product, and the stability of price levels and exchange rates. Monetary policy is directed by the Federal Reserve System. It functions by influencing the cost and availability of bank reserves through (1) open-market operations (the purchase and sale of securities, primarily Treasury securities), (2) changes in the ratio of reserves to deposits that commercial banks are required to maintain, and (3) changes in the discount rate. *(See also* Discount Rate; Fiscal Policy.)

MONEY SUPPLY (ECONOMICS TERM)

The Federal Reserve Board publishes the following measures of the money supply:

M1:   A relatively narrow measure of the U.S. money supply that primarily includes the public's (excluding the banks') holdings of currency, traveler's checks, and checking accounts.

M2:   A broader measure of the U.S. money supply than M1 that primarily includes M1 plus the public's holdings of (1) savings and small (less than $100,000) time deposit and money-market deposit accounts held at depositary institutions and (2) accounts at money-market mutual funds.

M3:   A much broader measure of the U.S. money supply that includes M2 plus large time deposits and term repurchase liabilities (in amounts of $100,000 or more), term Eurodollars, and balances in institution-only money market funds.

L: A broad measure of liquidity that includes M3 plus U.S. savings bonds, shortterm Treasury securities, commercial paper, and bankers acceptances.

Among these measures, M1 and M2 include assets that can most readily be used to make transactions or most easily be converted into those that can.

MONTHLY TREASURY STATEMENT (MTS)

A summary statement prepared from agency accounting reports and issued by the Department of the Treasury. The MTS presents the receipts, outlays, and resulting budget surplus or deficit, and federal debt for the month and the fiscal year-to date and compares those figures to the same period in the previous year. (*See also* Appendix to Treasury's Annual Report.)

MULTIYEAR BUDGET PLANNING

A process—such as the one used to develop the President's budget and the Congressional budget—designed to ensure that the long-range consequences of budget decisions are identified and reflected in the budget totals. The President's (or executive) budget includes multiyear planning estimates for budget authority, outlays, and receipts for 4 years beyond the budget year. The congressional budget process considers estimates covering a 3-year period. However, under the Budget Enforcement Act, congressional budgets cover a 5-year period. This process provides a structure for the review and analysis of long-term program and tax policy choices.

OMB planning estimates are either presidential policy or current services estimates. Presidential policy estimates represent projections or extrapolations of likely outcomes based upon current law and enunciated administration policy. In some cases, outyear presidential policy estimates represent outyear policy rather than an extrapolation from budget-year policy. Current services estimates represent projections of possible outcomes based on the continuation of existing levels of service without policy changes. *(See also* Current Services Estimates; Full Funding; Outyear; Projections.)

NATIONAL INCOME AND PRODUCT ACCOUNTS (ECONOMICS TERM)

Accounts prepared and published by the Department of Commerce that provide detailed quarterly and annual data on aggregate economic activity within the United States. These accounts depict in dollar terms the composition and use of the nation's output and the distribution of national income to different recipients. With a few exceptions, the output that is measured is the output acquired in market transactions by the final users. The accounts make it possible to measure aggregate output and income and trace trends and fluctuations in economic activity.

Because the national income and product accounts offer a consistent picture of the economy, they are basic analytical tools used to quantify past and present economic performance and also to forecast future economic developments. Furthermore, this quantitative framework increases the importance of these accounts to the formulation of national economic policies. *(See also* Gross Domestic Product.)

NATIONAL NEEDS

Broad areas providing a coherent and comprehensive basis for analyzing and understanding the budget in terms of the end purposes being served without regard to the means that may be chosen to meet those purposes. The budget resources devoted to meeting national needs are classified according to budget functions. In this way, budget authority and outlays of on-budget and off-budget federal entities, loan guarantees, and tax expenditures can be grouped in terms of the national needs being addressed. *(See also* Agency Mission; Functional Classification.)

NEW BUDGET AUTHORITY

Budget authority that first becomes available for obligation in a given fiscal year. This includes budget authority that becomes available as a result of a reappropriation or a statutory change in the availability of unobligated balances from a prior fiscal year. It also includes a change in the estimated level of indefinite budget authority. *(See also* Budget Authority.)

NEW SPENDING AUTHORITY

A term from the Congressional Budget Act (2 U.S.C. 651(c)) used in the congressional budget process for any statutory changes in permanent, contract, borrowing, or entitlement authority that would increase amounts otherwise available by law. *(See also* Congressional Budget Act; Spending Authority.)

NONBUDGETARY

A term used to refer to transactions of the government that do not belong within the budget. Nonbudgetary transactions (such as deposit funds, direct loan and loan guarantee financing accounts, and seigniorage) are outside the budget because they do not represent net budget authority or outlays, but rather are means of financing and do not belong within the budget. This contrasts with "off-budget," which refers to activities that are budgetary in nature but that are required by law to be excluded from the budget. *(See* Means of Financing.)

OBJECT CLASSIFICATION

A uniform classification identifying the obligations of the federal government by the types of goods or services purchased (such as personnel compensation, supplies and materials, and equipment) without regard to the agency involved or the purpose of the programs for which they are used. If the obligations are in a single object classification category, the classification is identified in the Program and Financing Schedule in the *Budget of the United States Government.* For the activities distributed among two or more object classification categories, the budget has a separate object classification schedule to show the distribution of the obligations by object classification. *(See also* Explanation of Estimates in the "Detailed Budget Estimates" section of the *Budget of the United States Government.* General instructions are provided in OMB Circular A-1 1, revised. *See also* Allocation. For a distinction, *see* Functional Classification.)

OBLIGATION LIMITATION

See under Limitation

OBLIGATIONAL AUTHORITY

The sum of (1) budget authority provided for a given fiscal year, (2) unobligated balances of amounts brought forward from prior years, (3) amounts of offsetting collections to be credited to specific funds or accounts during that year, and (4) transfers between funds or accounts. The balance of obligational authority is an amount carried over from one year to the next because not all obligational authority that becomes available in a fiscal year is obligated and paid out in that same year. Balances are described as (1) obligated, (2) unobligated, or (3) unexpended.

OBLIGATED BALANCE

The amount of obligations already incurred for which payment has not yet been made. For a fixed appropriation account, this balance can be carried forward and retains its fiscal year identity for five fiscal years after the period of availability ends. At the end of the fifth fiscal year, the account is closed and any remaining balance is canceled. Obligated balances of an appropriation account available for an indefinite period may be closed if (1) specifically rescinded by law, or (2) the head of the agency concerned or the President determines that the purposes for which the appropriation was made have been carried out and disbursements have not been made against the appropriation for 2 consecutive years. *(See also* Duration *under* Budget Authority; Fixed Appropriation Account.)

UNOBLIGATED BALANCE

The portion of obligational authority that has not yet been obligated. Unobligated balances whose period of availability has expired are not available for new obligation and may only be used for recording, adjusting, and liquidating obligations properly chargeable to the fiscal year account. For a fixed appropriation account, the balance can be carried forward for five fiscal years after the period of availability ends. At the end of the fifth fiscal year, the account is closed and any remaining balance is canceled. For a no-year account, the unobligated balance is carried forward indefinitely until (1) specifically rescinded by law, or (2) the head of the agency concerned or the President determines that the purposes for which the appropriation was made have been carried out and disbursements have not been made against the appropriation for 2 consecutive years. *(See also* Duration *under* Budget Authority; Expired Account; Expired Budget Authority *under* Availability for New Obligations *under* Budget Authority; Fixed Appropriation Account.)

UNEXPENDED BALANCE

The sum of the obligated and unobligated balances.

OBLIGATIONS INCURRED

Amounts of orders placed, contracts awarded, services received, and similar transactions during a given period that will require payments during the same or a future period. Such amounts will include outlays for which obligations have not been previously recorded and will reflect adjustments for differences between obligations previously recorded and actual outlays to liquidate those obligations. (For legal basis of obligations incurred, *see* 31 U.S.C. 1501-1502. *See also* OMB Circular A-34.)

OFF-BUDGET

The term refers to the status of transactions of the government (either federal funds or trust funds) that belong on-budget according to budget concepts but that are required by law to be excluded from the budget. The budget documents routinely report the on-budget and off-budget amounts separately and then add them together to arrive at the consolidated government totals. *(See also* Nonbudgetary; Off-Budget Federal Entity; Outlay; Trust Fund Expenditure Accounts *under* Trust Fund Accounts *under* Account in the President's Budget.)

OFF-BUDGET FEDERAL ENTITY

Any federal fund or trust fund whose transactions are required by law to be excluded from the totals of the President's budget and the Congress's budget resolutions, even though these are part of total government transactions. *(See* 2 U.S.C. 622(8).) Current law requires that the Social Security trust funds (the Federal Old Age and Survivors Insurance and the Federal Disability Insurance trust funds) and the Postal Service be off-budget. Currently these are the only offbudget entities; all other federal funds and trust funds are on-budget. Off-budget federal entities are discussed in the *Budget of the United States Government. (See also* Government-Sponsored Enterprise; Mixed-Ownership Government Corporation; Off-Budget; Total Deficit *under* Deficit; Wholly-Owned Government Corporation.)

ON-BUDGET

The term referring to transactions that are included within the budget.

OUTLAY

The issuance of checks, disbursement of cash, or electronic transfer of funds made to liquidate a federal obligation. Outlays also occur when interest on the Treasury debt held by the public accrues and when the government issues bonds, notes, debentures, monetary credits, or other cash-equivalent instruments in order to liquidate obligations. Also, under credit reform, the credit subsidy cost is recorded as an outlay when a direct or guaranteed loan is disbursed.

Outlays during a fiscal year may be for payment of obligations incurred in prior years (prior-year obligations) or in the same year. Outlays, therefore, flow in part from unexpended balances of prior-year budgetary resources and in part from budgetary resources provided for the year in which the money is spent.

Outlays are stated both gross and net of offsetting collections. *(See* Offsetting Collections *under* Collections.) Total government outlays include outlays of offbudget federal entities. *(See also* Expenditure; Expense.)

OUTYEAR

Any year (or years) beyond the budget year for which projections are made. For Budget Enforcement Act purposes, the term outyear means, with respect to a budget year, any of the fiscal years that follow the budget year through fiscal year 1995. *(See also* Multiyear Budget Planning.)

OVERSIGHT COMMITTEE

The congressional committee charged with general oversight of an agency's or program's operations. In most cases, the oversight committee for an agency or program is also its authorizing committee. The Senate Committee on Governmental Affairs and the House Committee on Government Operations also have general oversight on budget and accounting measures other than appropriations, except as provided in the Congressional Budget Act of 1974. *(See also* Authorizing Committee.)

PAY-AS-YOU-GO (BUDGET ENFORCEMENT ACT TERM)

Under the Budget Enforcement Act, the principle that all direct spending and tax legislation enacted after BEA for a fiscal year must be deficit-neutral in the aggregate. If Congress enacts direct spending or receipts legislation that causes a net increase in the deficit, it must offset that increase by either increasing revenues or decreasing another direct spending program in the same fiscal year. This requirement is enforced by sequestration. *(See also* Pay-As-You-Go Sequestration *under* Sequestration.)

PERFORMANCE BUDGETING

A measure of the efficiency and effectiveness of resource utilization by relating labor, material, and other costs provided for in a budget to defined results.

PERFORMANCE MEASUREMENT

Any systematic attempt to learn how responsive a government's services are to the needs of constituents through the use of standards and/or milestones.

POINT OF ORDER

An objection raised on the House or Senate floor or in committees to a motion or procedure that violates the body's rules. Gramm-Rudman-Hollings and the Budget Enforcement Act authorize points of order against legislation that would violate various budget resolutions or spending limits. Usually, a point of order may be waived by a simple majority vote. However, in the Senate, waiver of some points of order requires a three-fifths vote. *(See also* Concurrent Resolution on the Budget; Congressional Budget Act; Special Rules.)

PREPAYMENT OF A LOAN

See under Asset Sale/Loan Prepayment

PRESENT VALUE (ECONOMICS TERM)

The worth of a future stream of returns or costs in terms of money paid immediately (or at some designated date). A dollar available at some date in the future is worth less than a dollar available today because the latter could be invested at interest in the interim. In calculating present value, prevailing interest rates provide the basis for converting future amounts into their "money now" equivalents.

Under credit reform, the subsidy cost of direct loans and loan guarantees are to be computed on a present value basis and included as budget outlays at the time the direct or guaranteed loans are disbursed.

PRIME RATE (ECONOMICS TERM)

The rate of interest charged by commercial banks for short-term loans to highly creditworthy borrowers.

PRODUCER PRICE INDEXES (ECONOMICS TERM) (FORMERLY WHOLESALE PRICE INDEX)

A set of price measures for producers of commodities in the manufacturing, agriculture, forestry, fishing, mining, gas and electricity, and public utilities sectors. These indexes can be organized by either commodity or stage of processing and are published monthly by the Bureau of Labor Statistics. Changes from one month to another are usually expressed as either monthly or annualized percentage rates of change.

PROGRAM

Generally, an organized set of activities directed toward a common purpose or goal that an agency undertakes or proposes to carry out its responsibilities. Because the term has many uses in practice, it does not have a well-defined, standard meaning in the legislative process. It is used to describe an agency's mission, programs, functions, activities, services, projects, and processes. (*See also* Program, Project, or Activity.)

PROGRAM AND FINANCING SCHEDULE

A schedule published in the *Budget of the United States Government's* "Detailed Budget Estimates" presenting budget data by each appropriation or fund account. The schedule consists of three sections: (1) Program by Activities, (2) Financing, and (3) Relation of Obligations to Outlays.

PROGRAM EVALUATION

The application of scientific research methods to assess program concepts, implementation, and effectiveness. The primary focus of evaluation is on events and conditions that have (or are presumed to have) occurred or are being observed, not on what is likely to happen in the future. Despite the retrospective character of evaluation, program evaluation findings can often be used as a sound basis for calculating future costs or projecting the likely effects of a program..

PROGRAM, PROJECT, OR ACTIVITY (PPA)

An element within a budget account. For annually appropriated accounts, the PPAs are defined by the appropriations acts and accompanying reports and documentation; for accounts not funded by annual appropriations, they are defined by the program and financing schedules provided in the "Detailed Budget Estimates" in the *Budget of the United States Government* for the relevant fiscal year. Under sequestration procedures, except as specifically provided, PPAs are reduced by a uniform percentage.

PROJECTIONS

Estimates of budget authority, outlays, receipts, or other budget amounts extending several years into the future. Projections are generally intended to indicate the budgetary implications of existing or proposed programs and legislation. Projections may include alternative program and policy strategies and ranges of possible budget amounts. Projections usually are not firm estimates of what will occur in future years, nor are they intended to be recommendations for future budget decisions.

The statutory basis for preparing and submitting projections are spelled out (1) for the President in section 201 (a) of the Budget and Accounting Act (31 U.S.C. 1105), (2) for the Congress and Congressional Budget Office in sections 308 and 403 of the Congressional Budget and Impoundment Control Act (2 U.S.C. 639 and 653), and (3) for sequestration estimates in sections 251(a)(7), 252(d), and 257 of the Balanced Budget and Emergency Deficit Control Act, as amended, (2 U.S.C. 901(a)(7), 902(d), and 907). *(See also* Baseline; Budget Estimates; Multiyear Budget Planning.)

REAL ECONOMIC GROWTH

The increase in the gross domestic product, adjusted for inflation. For purposes of the Budget Enforcement Act, real economic growth must be determined in a way consistent with Department of Commerce definitions. (See also Low-Growth Report.)

REAPPORTIONMENT

A revision of a previous apportionment of budgetary resources for an appropriation or fund account. This revision must be approved by the Office of Management and Budget. Agencies usually submit requests for reapportionment to OMB as soon as a change becomes necessary due to changes in amounts available, program requirements, or cost factors. (For exceptions, *see* OMB Circular A-34, sec. 44.4.) This approved revision would ordinarily cover the same period, project, or activity covered in the original apportionment. (See also Allotment; Apportionment.)

RECEIPTS

See under Governmental Receipts *under* Collections

RECESSION (ECONOMICS TERM)

A pervasive, substantial decline in overall business activity that is of at least several months' duration. The National Bureau of Economic Research identifies recessions on the basis of several indicators. As a rule of thumb, recessions are commonly identified by a decline in real gross domestic product for at least two consecutive quarters.

RECONCILIATION

A process the Congress uses to reconcile amounts determined by tax, spending, credit, and debt legislation for a given fiscal year with levels set in the concurrent resolution on the budget for the year. Section 310 of the Congressional Budget and Impoundment Control Act of 1974 (2 U.S.C. 641) provides that the resolution may direct committees to determine and recommend changes to laws, bills, and resolutions as required to conform to totals for budget authority, revenues, and the public debt. Such changes are incorporated into either a reconciliation resolution or a reconciliation bill. *(See also* Concurrent Resolution on the Budget; Congressional Budget Act.)

RECONCILIATION BILL

A bill reported pursuant to reconciliation instructions in a congressional budget resolution changing enacted legislation. *(See also* Congressional Budget Act.)

RECONCILIATION INSTRUCTION

A provision in a concurrent resolution directing one or more committees to report (or submit to the Budget Committee) legislation changing existing laws or pending legislation in order to bring spending, revenues, or the debt limit into conformity with the budget resolution. The instructions specify the committees to which they apply, indicate the appropriate dollar changes to be achieved, and usually provide a deadline by which the legislation is to be reported or submitted.

RECONCILIATION RESOLUTION

A concurrent resolution (that the President does not sign) reported pursuant to reconciliation instructions in a congressional budget resolution directing the Clerk of the House of Representatives or the Secretary of the Senate to make specified changes in bills and resolutions that have not been enrolled.

REIMBURSEMENT

A sum (1) that is received by the federal government as a repayment for commodities sold or services furnished either to the public or to another government account and (2) that is authorized by law to be credited directly to specific appropriation and fund accounts. These amounts are deducted from the total obligations incurred (and outlays) in determining net obligations (and outlays) for such accounts. Reimbursements between two accounts for goods or services are an expenditure transaction/transfer.

Anticipated reimbursements are, in the case of transactions with the public, estimated collections of expected advances to be received or expected reimbursements to be earned. In transactions between government accounts, anticipated reimbursements consist of orders expected to be received for which no orders have been accepted. (See also Offsetting Collections under Collections; Unfilled Customer Orders.)

REOBLIGATION

Obligation of deobligated funds for another purpose. (See also Deobligation.)

REPROGRAMMING

Shifting funds within an appropriation or fund account to use them for different purposes than those contemplated at the time of appropriation (for example, obligating budgetary resources for a different object class from the one originally planned). While a transfer of funds involves shifting funds from one account to another, reprogramming involves shifting funds within an account.

Reprogramming is generally preceded by consultation between federal agencies and the appropriate congressional committees. It often involves formal notification and opportunity for congressional committees to state their approval or disapproval.

REQUIRED OUTLAY REDUCTION (GRAMM-RUDMAN-HOLLINGS TERM)

The total amount of outlays to be sequestered in a given fiscal year. The amount of excess deficit above the annual target. *(See also* Excess Deficit; Margin.)

RESCISSION

Legislation enacted by Congress that cancels the availability of budgetary resources previously provided by law before the authority would otherwise lapse.

The Impoundment Control Act of 1974 (2 U.S.C. 683) provides for the President to propose rescissions whenever the President determines that all or part of any budget authority will not be needed to carry out the full objectives or scope of programs for which the authority was provided. Likewise, a rescission will be proposed if all or part of any budget authority limited to a fiscal year—that is, annual appropriations or budget authority of a multiple-year appropriation in the last year of availability—is to be reserved from obligation for the entire fiscal year. Rescission of budget authority may also be proposed for fiscal policy or other reasons. Generally, amounts proposed for rescission are withheld for up to 45 calendar days of continuous session while the Congress considers the proposals.

All funds proposed for rescission, including those withheld, must be reported to the Congress in a special message. If both houses have not completed action on a rescission proposed by the President within 45 calendar days of continuous session, any funds being withheld must be made available for obligation. Congress may also initiate rescissions through its own appropriations process. Such congressional action occurs for various reasons, including changing priorities, program terminations, excessive unobligated balances, and program slippage. *(See also* Apportionment; Budgetary Reserves; Deferral of Budget Authority; Impoundment; Rescission Bill.)

RESCISSION BILL

A bill or joint resolution that cancels, in whole or in part, budget authority previously granted by law. Rescissions proposed by the President must be transmitted in a special message to the Congress. Under section 1012 of the Impoundment Control Act of 1974 (2 U.S.C. 683), unless both houses of the Congress complete action on a rescission bill within 45 calendar days of continuous session after receipt of the proposal, the budget authority must be made available for obligation. *(See also* Rescission.)

RESTORATION

An unobligated amount previously withdrawn (that is, transferred out of an appropriation account) by administrative action that is returned to the account and again made available for obligation and outlay. (For a distinction, *see* Reappropriation *under* Extensions of Budget Authority *under* Budget Authority.)

REVENUE

Either of the following:

(1) As used in the congressional budget process, a synonym for governmental receipts. Revenues result from amounts, such as receipts from individual income taxes, that are owed to the government but for which no current government action is required. Article I, section 7 of the U.S. Constitution requires that revenue bills originate in the House of Representatives.

(2) As used in an accounting sense, the increase in assets (or decrease in liabilities) that results from operations. Revenues result from (1) services performed by the federal government and (2) goods and other property delivered to purchasers. *(See* Collections.)

ROLLOVER

Instead of paying off a loan when due, the principal and sometimes accrued interest outstanding of a borrower is refinanced (rolled over) as a new loan with a new maturity date.

SCOREKEEPING

The process of estimating the budgetary effects of pending and enacted legislation and comparing them to limits set in the budget resolution or legislation. Scorekeeping tracks data such as budget authority, receipts, outlays, the surplus or deficit, and the public debt limit. For purposes of the Congressional Budget Process, the Budget Committees and the Congressional Budget Office are responsible for scoring legislation in relation to the levels set by the Congress in budget resolutions and the Budget Enforcement Act.

For purposes of sequestration, the Office of Management and Budget (OMB) scores legislation in relation to the spending limits, pay-as-you-go requirements, and the maximum deficit amounts established by the Budget Enforcement Act. If OMB determines through its scoring that legislation breaches the spending limits or the maximum deficit amount or does not meet the pay-as-you-go requirement for direct spending and receipts legislation, a sequester occurs.

Scorekeeping data published by CBO include, but are not limited to, status reports on the effects of congressional actions and comparisons of these actions to targets and ceilings set by the Congress in the budget resolutions. Weekly status reports are published in the *Congressional Record* for the Senate during the weeks it is in session and reports for the House of Representatives are published at least once monthly when the Congress is in session. CBO is required to produce periodic scorekeeping reports pursuant to section 308(b) of the Congressional Budget and Impoundment Control Act of 1974 (2 U.S.C. 639). Similarly, the Budget Enforcement Act requires OMB to submit to Congress, five days after enactment, the budget impact of any appropriation, direct spending, or receipts legislation. OMB must also make reports to Congress with the submission of the budget, on August 20th, and 15 days after the end of a congressional session.

The joint explanatory statement of managers accompanying the conference report on the Omnibus Budget Reconciliation Act of 1990 contains guidelines that the Budget Committees, CBO and OMB use to score legislation. (*See also* Current Level Estimates.)

SEIGNIORAGE

The difference between the face value of minted coins and the cost of their production, including the cost of metal used in the minting. Seigniorage is recorded as general fund revenue resulting from an increase in the value of government assets when coinage metal is converted to a coin whose face value is higher than the cost of the metal. Seigniorage arises from the government's exercise of its monetary powers. In contrast to receipts from the public, it involves no corresponding payment by another party. For budget reporting purposes, seigniorage is excluded from receipts and treated as a means of financing a deficit—other than borrowing from the public—or as a supplementary amount that can be applied to reduce debt or to increase the Treasury's cash when there is a budget surplus. *(See also* Means of Financing.)

SEQUESTER

See under Sequestration

SEQUESTRABLE RESOURCE

Budgetary resources subject to reduction or cancellation under a presidential sequester order. Sequestrable budgetary resources are new budget authority unobligated balances, direct spending authority, and obligation limitations. Certain programs are exempt from sequestration under the Budget Enforcement Act. *(See also* Entitlement Authority; Exempt Programs and Activities; Gramm-Rudman-Hollings; Sequestration; Special Rules.)

SEQUESTRATION (BUDGET ENFORCEMENT ACT TERM)

The cancellation, in accordance with the Budget Enforcement Act, of budgetary resources provided by discretionary appropriations or direct spending law. The Budget Enforcement Act created three types of sequestration-discretionary spending sequestration, pay-as-you-go sequestration, and deficit-reduction sequestration. (*See also* Automatic Spending Increase; Budgetary Resources; Category of Discretionary Spending; Excess Deficit; Gramm-Rudman-Hollings; Impoundment;

Margin; Maximum Deficit Amount; Rescission; Sequestrable Resource; Special Rules; Uniform Reduction Percentage.)

DISCRETIONARY SPENDING SEQUESTRATION

Sequestration designed to prevent spending from exceeding the discretionary spending limits set by the Budget Enforcement Act and adjusted by OMB for specific reasons provided by law. The timing of such a sequestration depends on when the appropriations that cause the limits to be exceeded are enacted.

(1) An end-of-session sequestration occurs within 15 days after Congress adjourns to end a session, if appropriations enacted before Congress adjourns cause a breach in the limits for that fiscal year.

(2) If an appropriation is enacted during the next session of Congress (after Congress adjourns to end the session for the budget year), but before July 1, that causes a breach in the limits for that fiscal year, a within-session sequestration occurs 15 days later.

If an appropriation is enacted between June 30 and September 30 for the fiscal year in progress that causes a breach in a spending limit, the applicable spending limit for the next fiscal year is reduced by the amount of the breach.

PAY-AS-YOU-GO SEQUESTRATION

Sequestration of direct spending programs required if direct spending or receipts legislation enacted subsequent to the enactment of BEA causes a net increase in the deficit. Pay-as-you-go sequestrations are always end-of-session sequestrations.

DEFICIT-REDUCTION SEQUESTRATION

Sequestration resembling the Gramm-Rudman-Hollings sequestration in that it is designed to eliminate the overall excess deficit. However, provisions for a deficit reduction sequestration are designed so that there should be no deficit-reduction sequestration necessary for fiscal years 1991 through 1993. For fiscal years 1994 and 1995, the President may choose to adjust the maximum deficit amount to reflect up-to-date reestimates of economic and technical assumptions. If he does so, a deficit-reduction sequestration should not be necessary.

SEQUESTRATION REPORTS (BUDGET ENFORCEMENT ACT TERM)

Reports issued by CBO and OMB to the Congress on Budget Enforcement Act consequences of legislation and indicating the necessity for a sequestration.

SEQUESTRATION REPORTS CLASSIFIED BY CONTENT

Discretionary Sequestration Report.

A sequestration report setting forth, in the preview and update reports, estimates for the current year and each subsequent year through 1995 of the applicable spending limits for each category and an explanation of any adjustments in such limits.

The final report also includes a discretionary sequestration report that sets forth estimates (1) for the current year and the budget year, the estimated new budget authority and outlays for each category and the breach, if any, in each category; (2) for each category for which a sequestration is required, the sequestration percentages necessary to achieve the required reduction; and (3) for the budget year, for each account to be sequestered, estimates of the baseline level of sequestrable budgetary resources and resulting outlays and the amount of budgetary resources to be sequestered and resulting outlay reductions. (See also Adjustments to Discretionary Spending Limits; Breach; Discretionary; Sequestration; Sequestration Reports Classified by Timing.)

Pay as You-Go Sequestration Report.

A sequestration report containing, in the preview and update reports, the following: (1) the amount of net deficit increase or decrease, if any, calculated under pay-as-you-go look-back procedures; (2) a list identifying each law enacted and sequestration implemented (after the date of enactment of the Budget Enforcement Act) included in the calculation of the amount of deficit increase or decrease with a specification of the budgetary effect of each such law; and (3) the sequestration percentage or percentage necessary to prevent a deficit increase.

The final pay-as-you-go sequestration report contains (1) all of the information required in the preview report; (2) for the budget year, for each account to be sequestered, estimates of the baseline level of sequestrable budgetary resources and resulting outlays and the amount of budgetary resources to be sequestered and resulting outlay reductions; and (3) estimates of the effects on outlays of the sequestration in each outyear through 1995 for direct spending programs. (*See also* Look-Back; Pay-As-You-Go; Sequestration Reports Classified by Timing.)

Deficit Sequestration Report.

A sequestration report containing, in the preview and update reports, the following: (1) the maximum deficit amount, the estimated deficit, the amount by which the estimated exceeds the maximum deficit (the excess deficit), and the margin, (2) the amount of required pay-as-you go reductions, the excess deficit remaining after those reductions have been made, and the amount of additional reductions required from defense and nondefense accounts.

The final deficit sequestration report contains (1) all of the information required in the preview report, (2) for the budget year, for each account to be sequestered, estimates of the baseline level of sequestrable budgetary resources and resulting outlays and the amount of budgetary resources to be sequestered and resulting outlay reductions, and (3) estimates of the effects on outlays of the sequestration in each outyear through 1995 for direct spending programs. (*See also* Sequestration Reports Classified by Timing.)

SEQUESTRATION REPORTS CLASSIFIED BY TIMING

Preview Reports.

Discretionary, pay-as-you-go, and deficit sequestration reports issued by OMB and CBO based upon laws enacted through their issuance dates. CBO issues its preview report five days before the President's annual budget submission to the Congress. OMB issues its preview report the day of the President's budget submission. CBO issues its report to OMB, the Senate, and the House of Representatives and OMB issues its report to the Senate, the House of Representatives, and the President. (*See also* Sequestration Reports Classified by Content.)

Sequestration Update Reports.

Deficit, discretionary, and pay-as-you-go reports issued on August 15 by CBO to OMB, the House of Representatives, and the Senate and by OMB on August 20 to the President, the House of Representatives, and the Senate. These reports are to reflect laws enacted through those dates and must contain all the information required in the sequestration preview reports. *(See also* Sequestration Reports Classified by Content.)

Within-Session Sequestration Report.

Discretionary sequestration reports that are issued by CBO and OMB 10 and 15 days respectively, after enactment of an appropriation for a fiscal year in progress that causes a breach of discretionary spending limits, if the Congress enacts such appropriations after the Congress adjourns to end the session for that budget year and before July 1 of that fiscal year. *(See also* Sequestration Reports Classified by Content.)

Final Sequestration Reports.

Deficit, discretionary, and pay-as-you-go reports issued 10 days after the end of a congressional session by CBO to OMB, the House of Representatives, and the Senate and by OMB 15 days after the end of session to the President, the House of Representatives, and the Senate. These reports reflect laws enacted through their dates of issuance and contain all information contained in the preview reports as well as additional information on sequestrations if necessary. *(See also* Sequestration Reports Classified by Content.)

SPECIAL FUND ACCOUNTS

See under Federal Fund Accounts *under* Account in the President's Budget

SPECIAL RULES (BUDGET ENFORCEMENT ACT TERM)

Either of the following:

(1) Procedures for calculating the sequestrable amount for certain programs that yield sequestration reductions different from the

uniform percentage reduction. For example, the sequestration of Medicare to enforce deficit targets is limited by a special rule to not more than 2 percent, although the uniform percentage reduction may be higher. *(See also* Automatic Spending Increase; Sequestrable Resource; Sequestration; Uniform Reduction Percentage.)

(2) Procedures, usually in the House of Representatives, waiving points of order against legislation that violates procedural or substantive restrictions in the Congressional Budget Act of 1974 (2 U.S.C. 601-661). *(See also* Congressional Budget Act; Point of Order.)

SPENDING AUTHORITY

As defined by section 401(c) of the Congressional Budget Act of 1974, as amended (2 U.S.C. 651(c)), a collective designation for authority provided in laws other than appropriation acts to obligate the government to make payments. It includes contract authority, authority to borrow, and entitlement authority for which the budget authority is not provided in advance by appropriation acts. It also includes authority to forgo the collection of proprietary offsetting receipts and to make any other payments for which the budget authority is not provided in advance by appropriation acts. Spending authority is commonly referred to as backdoor authority or 401(c) authority. *(See also* Backdoor Authority/Backdoor Spending; Congressional Budget Act; Direct Spending Authority; Entitlement Authority; New Spending Authority; Spending Committee.)

SPENDING COMMITTEE

A standing committee of the House or Senate with jurisdiction over legislation permitting the obligation of funds. The House and Senate Appropriations Committees are spending committees for discretionary programs. For other programs, the authorizing legislation itself permits the obligation of funds (backdoor authority). In that case, the authorizing committees are the spending committees. *(See also* Authorizing Committee; Backdoor Authority/Backdoor Spending; Spending Authority.)

SPENDOUT RATE/OUTLAY RATE

In a fiscal year, the ratio of outlays resulting from new budgetary resources to the new budgetary resources. The two terms are synonymous. *(See also* Composite Outlay Rate.)

STANDARD GENERAL LEDGER
CHART OF ACCOUNTS

A uniform listing of accounts and supporting transactions that standardizes federal agency accounting and supports the preparation of standard external reports. The U.S. Government Standard General Ledger Chart of Accounts

(1) provides control over all financial transactions and resource balances,
(2) satisfies basic reporting requirements of OMB and Treasury, and
(3) integrates proprietary and budgetary accounting.

STANDARDIZED EMPLOYMENT BUDGET
(ECONOMICS TERM)

A budget that removes the influence of economic fluctuations by calculating the level of receipts and expenditures that would occur under current law if economic activity were equal to some estimate of the economy's high-employment potential.

STRUCTURAL DEFICIT

The portion of the budget deficit that would remain even if the unemployment rate were at the inflation threshold level (that is, the lowest level of unemployment possible without increasing inflation). (*See also* High Employment Budget.)

SUBFUNCTION

A subdivision of a budget function. For example, health care services and health research are subfunctions of the health budget function.

SUBSIDY

Generally, a payment or benefit made by the federal government where the benefit exceeds the cost to the beneficiary. Subsidies are designed to support the conduct of an economic enterprise or activity, such as ship operations. They may also refer to (1) provisions in the tax laws for certain tax expenditures and (2) the provision of loans, goods, and services to the public at prices lower than market value. These include interest subsidies.

Under credit reform, the net present value of the cost to the government of direct loans or loan guarantees constitute subsidies. *(See also* Credit Reform; Credit Subsidy Cost; Tax Expenditure.)

SUBSTANTIVE LAW

A law that usually authorizes the executive branch to carry out a program of work or activity or that creates rights and obligations. Financing of the program is usually provided through permanent or annual appropriations. *(See also* Authorizing Legislation.)

SUPPLEMENTAL APPROPRIATION

An act appropriating funds in addition to those in an annual appropriation act. Supplemental appropriations provide additional budget authority beyond the original estimates for programs or activities (including new programs authorized after the date of the original appropriation act) in cases where the need for funds is too urgent to be postponed until enactment of the regular appropriation bill. Supplementals may sometimes include items not appropriated in the regular bills for lack of timely authorizations.

SURPLUS

BUDGET SURPLUS

The amount by which the government's budget receipts exceed its budget outlays for a given period, usually a fiscal year. Sometimes a deficit is a negative surplus.

TOTAL SURPLUS

The amount by which the sum of the government's on-budget and off-budget receipts exceed the sum of its on-budget and off-budget outlays for a given period, usually a fiscal year. *(See also* Total Deficit *under Deficit.)*

SUSPENSE ACCOUNT

A combined receipt and expenditure account established to temporarily hold funds which are later refunded or paid into another government fund when an administrative or final determination as to the proper disposition is made.

SUSPENSION OF SEQUESTRATION PROCEDURES

The temporary cancellation of sequestration procedures. The issuance of a low growth report triggers the process to suspend Budget Enforcement Act sequestration provisions and certain Budget Enforcement Act points of order by requiring the Senate Majority Leader to introduce a joint resolution to suspend portions of the act and permitting the House Majority Leader to introduce a similar resolution. Enactment of a declaration of war would automatically suspend the sequestration process and certain Budget Enforcement Act points of order. *(See also Low* Growth Report.)

TAX

A sum that a government authority imposes upon persons or property to pay for government activities.

The power to impose and collect federal taxes is given to the Congress in Article I, Section 8 of the Constitution. Collections that arise from the sovereign powers of the federal government constitute the bulk of governmental receipts, which are compared with budget outlays in calculating the budget surplus or deficit. *(See also* Governmental Receipts *under* Collections; Revenue.)

TAX CREDIT

An amount that offsets or reduces tax liability. When the allowable tax credit amount exceeds the tax liability, and the difference is paid to the taxpayer, the credit is considered refundable. Otherwise, the difference can be (1) allowed as a carryforward against future tax liability, (2) allowed as a carryback against past taxes paid, or (3) lost as a tax benefit. *(See also* Tax Expenditure.)

TAX DEDUCTION

An amount that is subtracted from the tax base before tax liability is calculated.

TAX EXPENDITURE

A revenue loss attributable to a provision of the federal tax laws that (1) allows a special exclusion, exemption, or deduction from gross income or (2) provides a special credit, preferential tax rate, or deferral of tax liability.

Tax expenditures are subsidies provided through the tax system. Rather than transferring funds from the government to the private sector, the U.S. Treasury Department forgoes some of the receipts that it would have collected, and the beneficiary taxpayers pay lower taxes than they would have had to pay. Examples include tax expenditures for child care and the exclusion of fringe benefits from taxation. *(See also* Subsidy; Tax Credit; Tax Expenditures Budget.)

TAX EXPENDITURES BUDGET

A list of legally sanctioned tax expenditures for each fiscal year and an estimate of revenue loss which, according to the 1974 Congressional Budget and Impoundment Control Act, as amended (31 U.S.C. 1105 (a)(16)), must be part of the President's budget submission to the Congress. The Tax Expenditures Budget is for display purposes only and is not a budget that allocates these tax expenditures annually. *(See also* Tax Expenditure.)

TECHNICAL AND ECONOMIC ASSUMPTIONS

Assumptions about factors affecting estimations of future outlays and receipts that are not a direct function of legislation. Economic assumptions involve such factors as the future inflation and interest rates. Technical assumptions involve all other nonpolicy factors. For example, in the Medicare program, estimations regarding demography, hospitalization versus out-patient treatment, and morbidity all affect estimations of future outlays. *(See also* Adjustments to Maximum Deficit Amount.)

TRANSFER

Shifting of all or part of the budget authority in one appropriation or fund account to another, as specifically authorized by law. The nature of the transfer determines whether the transaction is treated as an expenditure or a nonexpenditure transfer. *(See also* Allocation.)

EXPENDITURE TRANSFER

A transaction between appropriation and fund accounts which represents payments, repayments, or receipts for goods or services furnished or to be furnished.

Where the purpose is to purchase goods or services or otherwise benefit the transferring account, an expenditure transfer/transaction is recorded as an obligation/outlay in the transferring account and an offsetting collection in the receiving accounts.

If the receiving account is a general fund appropriation account or a revolving fund account, the offsetting collection is credited to the appropriation or fund account. If the receiving account is a special fund or trust account, the offsetting collection is usually credited to a receipt account of the fund.

All transfers between federal funds (general, special, and nontrust revolving funds) and trust funds are also treated as expenditure transfers.

NONEXPENDITURE TRANSFER

For accounting and reporting purposes, a transaction between appropriation and fund accounts that does not represent payments for goods and services received or to be received but rather serves only to adjust the amounts available in the accounts for making payments. However, transactions between budget accounts and deposit funds will always be treated as expenditure transactions since the deposit funds are outside the budget. Nonexpenditure transfers also include allocations. These transfers may not be recorded as obligations or outlays of the transferring accounts or as reimbursements or receipts of the receiving accounts. For example, the transfer of budget authority from one account to another to absorb the cost of a federal pay raise is a nonexpenditure transfer. *(See* Allocation; *see also* Transfer Appropriation Accounts *under* Account for Purposes Other Than Budget Presentation.)

TRANSFER PAYMENT (ECONOMICS TERM)

In the national income and product accounts, a payment made by the federal government or a business firm to an individual or organization for which no current or future goods or services are required in return. Government transfer payments include Social Security benefits, unemployment insurance benefits, government retirement benefits, and welfare payments. Transfer payments by business firms consist mainly of gifts to nonprofit institutions. Businesses also commonly include as transfer payments customer debts that remain unpaid and are thus considered bad debts. (*See also* National Income and Product Accounts.)

TREASURY SECURITY

A debt instrument of the U.S. Treasury issued to finance the operations of the government or refinance the government's debt.

TREASURY BILL

The shortest term federal security. Maturity dates for Treasury bills normally vary from 3 to 12 months and are sold at a discount from face value rather than carrying a coupon rate of interest.

TREASURY NOTE

A federal debt instrument with a maturity from 1 to 10 years.

TREASURY BOND

A federal debt instrument with a maturity of more than 10 years.

TRUST FUND ACCOUNTS

See under Account in the President's Budget

UNDELIVERED ORDERS

The value of goods and services ordered and obligated which have not been received. This amount includes any orders for which advance payment has been made but for which delivery or performance has not yet occurred. This term is synonymous with unliquidated obligations. (*See also* Advance.)

UNDISTRIBUTED OFFSETTING RECEIPTS

Offsetting receipts that are deducted from totals for the government as a whole rather than from a single agency or subfunction in order to avoid distortion of agency or subfunction totals. Offsetting receipts that are undistributed in both agency and functional tables are the collections of employer share of employee retirement payments, rents and royalties on the Outer Continental Shelf, and the sales of major assets.

Interest received by trust funds are undistributed offsetting receipts in the agency tables, but are distributed by function (that is, they are subfunctions 902 and 903 in functional tables). (For a more detailed description, *see* "Federal Programs by Function" and the introduction to "Technical Perspectives on Expenditures, OffBudget Activities, Capital Outlays, and Borrowing" in the *Budget of the United States Government.)*

UNEMPLOYMENT RATE (ECONOMICS TERM)

The share of the labor force that is unemployed. It is the number of unemployed persons, most commonly expressed as a percentage of the civilian labor force but sometimes as a percentage of other relevant labor forces or of the total labor force, including the armed forces residing in the United States.

UNFILLED CUSTOMER ORDERS

The dollar amount of orders accepted from other accounts within the government for goods and services to be furnished on a reimbursable basis. In the case of transactions with the public, these orders are amounts advanced or collected for which the account or fund has not yet performed the service or incurred its own obligations for that purpose. *(See also* Reimbursements *under* Offsetting Collections *under* Collections.)

UNIFIED BUDGET

Under budget concepts set forth in the *Report of the President's Commission on Budget Concepts,* a comprehensive budget in which receipts and outlays from federal and trust funds are consolidated. When these fund groups are consolidated to display budget totals, transactions that are outlays of one fund group for payment to the other fund group (that is, interfund transactions) are deducted to avoid double counting. The unified budget should, as conceived by the President's Commission, be comprehensive of the full range of federal activities. However, by law, budget authority, outlays, and receipts of off-budget programs (currently only the U.S. Postal Service and Social Security) are excluded from the current budget, but data relating to off-budget programs are displayed in the budget documents.

UNIFORM REDUCTION PERCENTAGE (BUDGET ENFORCEMENT ACT TERM)

The proportion of accounts to be sequestered. For most sequestrable budgetary resources, the amount to be sequestered is determined by multiplying the amount included in the baseline for that resource by the defense or nondefense uniform reduction percentage. For some programs with automatic spending increases or covered by special rules in Gramm-Rudman-Hollings, as amended by the Budget Enforcement Act, special procedures for calculating sequestrable amounts are applied. *(See also* Automatic Spending Increase; Sequestrable Resource; Sequestration. For exceptions to the uniform reduction percentage, *see* Special Rules.)

UP-TO-DATE (BUDGET ENFORCEMENT ACT TERM)

The most recent generally accepted concept, definition, estimate, or other budgetary information. Up-to-date usually refers to what is accepted in the Congress; however, it is not specifically defined in BEA. *(See also* Adjustment to Maximum Deficit Amount. For a distinction, *see* Current.)

USER FEE

A fee charged to users for goods or services provided by the federal government. User fees generally apply to federal activities that provide special benefits to identifiable recipients above and beyond what is normally available to the public. User fees are normally related to the cost of the goods or services provided. They may be paid into the general fund or, under specific statutory authority, may be made available to an agency carrying out the activity. An example is a fee for entering a national park.

From an economic point of view, user fees may also be collected through a tax such as an excise tax. Since these collections result from the government's sovereign powers, the proceeds are recorded as budget receipts, not as offsetting receipts or offsetting collections.

In the narrow budgetary sense, a toll for the use of a highway is considered a user fee because it is related to the specific use of a particular section of highway. Such a fee would be counted as an offsetting receipt or collection and might be available for use by the agency. Alternatively, highway excise taxes on gasoline are considered a form of user charge in the economic sense, but since the tax must be paid regardless of how the gasoline is used and since it is not directly linked with the provision of the specific service, it is considered a tax and is recorded as a governmental receipt in the budget. *(See also* Offsetting Collections *under* Collections; Tax.)

VIEWS AND ESTIMATES REPORT

A report that the Congressional Budget Act of 1974 requires each House and Senate committee with jurisdiction over federal programs to submit to their respective Budget Committees each year within 6 weeks of the submission of the President's budget. Each report contains a committee's comments or recommendations on budgetary matters within its jurisdiction.

WARRANT

An official document that the Secretary of the Treasury issues pursuant to law and that establishes the amount of monies authorized to be withdrawn from the central accounts that Treasury maintains. Warrants for currently unavailable special and trust fund receipts are issued when requirements for their availability have been met. (For a discussion of availability, *see* Availability for New Obligations *under* Budget Authority.)

WHOLESALE PRICE INDEX

See under Producer Price Indexes

WHOLLY-OWNED GOVERNMENT CORPORATION

An enterprise or business activity established by statute and designated as a wholly-owned government corporation. Each such corporation is required to submit an annual business-type statement to the Office of Management and Budget. Wholly-owned government corporations are audited by the General Accounting Office as required by the Government Corporation Control Act of 1945, as amended (31 U.S.C. 9105) and other laws. The Pension Benefit Guaranty Corporation is an example of a wholly-owned government corporation. Budget concepts call for any corporation that is wholly owned by the government to be included on-budget. *(See also* Government-Sponsored Enterprise, Mixed-Ownership Government Corporation; Off-Budget Federal Entity.)

WORKING CAPITAL FUND

A revolving fund that operates as an accounting entity. In these funds, the assets are capitalized and all income is in the form of offsetting collections derived from the funds' operations and available in their entirety to finance the funds' continuing cycle of operations without fiscal year limitation. A working capital fund is a type of intragovernmental revolving fund. *(See also* Intragovernmental Revolving Fund Account *under* Intragovernmental Fund Accounts *under* Account in the President's Budget.)

SUBJECT INDEX